America's Favorite Holidays

The publisher gratefully acknowledges the generous support of the Chairman's Circle of the University of California Press Foundation, whose members are:

Stephen A. & Melva Arditti
Elizabeth & David Birka-White
Judith L. Hopkinson
Ajay Shah & Lata Krishnan
Barbara Z. Otto
Peter J. & Chinami S. Stern
Lynne Withey

America's Favorite Holidays

Candid Histories

BRUCE DAVID FORBES

UNIVERSITY OF CALIFORNIA PRESS

University of California Press, one of the most distinguished university presses in the United States, enriches lives around the world by advancing scholarship in the humanities, social sciences, and natural sciences. Its activities are supported by the UC Press Foundation and by philanthropic contributions from individuals and institutions. For more information, visit www.ucpress.edu.

University of California Press
Oakland, California

Frontispiece: Housewife with turkey, 1940s. Courtesy of the Graphics Fairy, www.thegraphicsfairy.com.

Library of Congress Cataloging-in-Publication Data

Forbes, Bruce David, author.
    America's favorite holidays : candid histories / Bruce David Forbes.
        pages   cm
    Includes bibliographical references and index.
    ISBN 978-0-520-28471-5 (cloth : alk. paper) —
    ISBN 978-0-520-28472-2 (pbk. : alk. paper) —
    ISBN 978-0-520-96044-2 (ebook)
    1. Holidays—United States—History.   I. Title.
    GT4803.F67   2015
    394.26973—dc23   2015016335

Manufactured in the United States of America

24   23   22   21   20   19   18   17   16   15
10   9   8   7   6   5   4   3   2   1

The paper used in this publication meets the minimum requirements of ANSI/NISO Z39.48-1992 (R 2002) (Permanence of Paper).

CONTENTS

ACKNOWLEDGMENTS

My interest in these holidays has been percolating for several years, and I am thankful to so many people who have helped along the way. Morningside College President John Reynders and Provost William Deeds granted me a sabbatical that provided much invaluable time for research and writing. Administrative Assistant Sherry Swan constantly and graciously goes above and beyond in more ways than I can count. Colleagues, students, and friends who have responded to portions of the manuscript, assisted in digging out information, or helped me think through concepts and issues include Pat Bass, Steve Coyne, Marty Knepper, Guy Greene, Barry Cytron, Gene Galla-gher, Amy Frykholm, Jessica Tinklenberg, Robert Jewett, Jim Stroh, Doug Livermore, Adam Fullerton, Karen Johnson, Doug Collins, Lindsey West-brook, Rusty and Lynette Brace, Corinne Schuster, Tammy and Al Huf, Beth Bailey, Cathy Wurzer, Martha Sawyer Allen, Margaret Thomas, and Sandra DiNanni.

Editors Eric Schmidt and Dore Brown, copy editor Jan Spauschus, and numerous staff at the University of California Press have been enthusiastic, patient, and indispensable in bringing this book to publication.

As always, I am most thankful to my son Matthew; in addition to the close bond we share, as a lawyer he also happens to be an exceptionally impressive researcher and dialogue partner.

Introduction

Some holiday snippets:

+ Several years ago I returned from a Labor Day weekend trip to find that while I was away, one house in my neighborhood had been decorated with Halloween lights and inflatable ghosts and pumpkins. Over the Labor Day weekend! People sometimes complain that Christmas lights go up too early, but this was new. Halloween decorations already?

+ At a Thanksgiving dinner gathering of several families, casual conversation at the tables stopped when a little boy seated next to me blurted out, in full voice, "I get it! All my favorite days have fancy food!" Many laughed, and his mother smiled.

+ A college student in one of my classes learned that her best friend had become engaged on Valentine's Day. She confided to me that if her boyfriend ever tried the same thing on Valentine's Day she would tell him no, and to try again. Everyone gets engaged on that day, she said, and she wanted her proposal to be special, on some other day of the year.

+ One Easter, while visiting my son in Washington, DC, we attended Sunday worship at a prominent local church. A mother and two teenage daughters seated behind us all wore very attractive spring hats. "Easter bonnets," I thought to myself. "How long has it been since I've seen one of those?"

+ A little ceramic figurine sits on my office desk, a gift from a friend. It combines two whimsical figures, an Easter Bunny handing a decorated egg to Santa Claus. I have no idea what it means. If anything.

So many holidays, so many memories. And for me, so much curiosity. How did these holidays get to be the way they are today?

I am first of all a participant in these holidays, along with my family and friends. For me the days evoke childhood memories—of Christmas carols, and Valentine boxes in grade school, and Easter egg decorations, and Halloween costumes, and school Thanksgiving pageants about Pilgrims and Indians, and family meals, and worship services, and candy, and presents. Since then there have been many additional adult experiences—meaningful moments, funny stories, big surprises, and touching events. There also are frustrations. As I grow older, some holidays have changed in ways I do not especially like. Family gatherings both expand and decline. Children grow up and have families of their own, adding new excitement when babies arrive, but they also gain new obligations to in-laws and sometimes move far away. Loved ones die, and family gatherings may not be as large as they used to be. The surrounding culture also changes, in all kinds of ways, and there is exasperation about religious meanings, commercialization, hectic schedules, and exhausting pressures.

In addition to being a participant, I also am a college professor of religious studies, with special interests in the history of Christianity, the history of American religions of all kinds, and the analysis of popular culture, especially the ways that religions and cultures intertwine. So, as I experience the holidays that I love, I also can't help growing curious about where they came from, how they developed, and what they mean. In many cases I suspect that the conventional stories we hear are sugarcoated or even flat-out inaccurate, and I became interested in investigating on my own, consulting various academic sources. I want to know the real stories.

When it comes down to it, though, I know that this curiosity is not limited to college professors. As children, most of us gladly celebrate major holidays and spend little time wondering about their origins. Yet we eventually want to learn more, especially when we encounter questions about particular days. Was Christmas always as commercialized as it is today? Is Thanksgiving a religious holiday or a secular holiday? Should Christians oppose Halloween as something threatening to their religion?

My casual investigations became more formal when, several years ago, the choir director at my school, Morningside College, decided to expand the annual evening Christmas concert into a full day of activities, with a craft fair, Scandinavian folk dancers, an elaborate holiday meal, and more. He asked if I could do an illustrated talk about the history of Christmas, and I agreed. When I began my formal research, I was immediately fascinated by all the surprises. For instance, I did not know that the earliest Christians had no celebration of the nativity of Jesus, or that St. Nick is an elf in the famous poem "The Night Before Christmas," not the way he is pictured in most children's storybooks. The audience was enthusiastic about the presentation and several people encouraged me to make it available in written form. The result, several years later, was *Christmas: A Candid History*, first published in 2007. It was written for general readers; I was guided by the words of a friend who told me that while he was interested in an overall history of how Christmas developed, he did not want to read a four-hundred-page volume or, worse, a list of ten books. As he remarked, "I'm curious, but I'm not obsessed." That book was written for people like him. And so is this one.

After the success of the Christmas book, readers asked if I planned to write another volume about some other holiday. I said no, because no other American holiday is as big as Christmas. However, people seemed to assume that if I knew something about the history of Christmas I must be knowledgeable about additional holidays as well, and I soon found myself doing interviews about Halloween or Valentine's Day, often woefully underprepared. The fascination kicked in again. Not only did I find the history of these additional holidays intriguing and full of surprises, but I also started to notice common patterns. For example, I was aware of academic discussions about the domestication of Christmas, in which cultural leaders worked to eliminate rowdy elements and make it safer and more appropriate for families and children, but I began to discover that something very similar happened with other holidays as well.

This book is the result, with a chapter on each of five holidays: Christmas, Valentine's Day, Easter, Halloween, and Thanksgiving. They are simply my choices, my focus at the moment. The fact that I am a religious studies professor undoubtedly has influenced my selection of holidays, because my academic background allows me to bring something to the discussion when there is at least a touch of religion involved (which is more obvious in some cases than others).

In addition, however, I think one could argue that these are the five most culturally dominant holidays in the United States, and thus of interest to the greatest number of people. If you use the word "America" as a synonym for the United States, these might be called America's five favorite holidays. Making lists of favorites is fashionable these days: the twelve best vacation destinations, the top one hundred movies of all time, the ten best-dressed celebrities at the Oscars, or America's twenty most livable cities. When anyone makes a list, the rest of us join in with our own choices that vary from the list, a sport that is both understandable and fun. So I understand if others have their own ideas about what America's five favorite holidays might be. One measure of popularity could be consumer spending, and the five days featured in this book are all near the top of "America's Consumer Holidays" as listed by the National Retail Federation (admittedly mixed in with back-to-school shopping and the Super Bowl).[1] Two of the holidays, Thanksgiving and Easter, ironically seem to have receded commercially in recent years, but they still rank high, and for huge numbers of people in the United States they remain especially important times for gatherings of family and friends. Many businesses still close on those two days, and college students and military personnel frequently express special regret and loneliness when they are unable to return home for Thanksgiving and Easter.

Recently I stumbled upon an amusing confirmation of the choice of these five holidays from an unanticipated source. Five or six years after I began thinking about this project and chose these five holidays as my focus, a friend gave me a Hallmark-published gift book featuring the Peanuts comic strip characters. Titled *Holidays through the Year: Five Classic Stories*, it contains storybook adaptations of five of the Peanuts television specials pertaining to holidays.[2] The first and best known television special was *A Charlie Brown Christmas*, which surprised skeptical network executives when half of the television sets in the United States tuned in for its initial broadcast in 1965.[3] Thereafter producer Lee Mendelson and animator Bill Melendez worked with Peanuts creator Charles Schultz to develop sixty-two additional television specials over almost forty years, about ten of which were holiday related, especially to Christmas. In addition to the Christmas classic, the other four specials included in the gift book are

It's the Great Pumpkin, Charlie Brown

A Charlie Brown Thanksgiving

Be My Valentine, Charlie Brown

It's the Easter Beagle, Charlie Brown

Yes, the five holidays featured in that gift book are the very same ones I had been considering for several years. This does not prove anything, but it's nice to know that others have similar inclinations.

Introduction

I am very aware that concentrating on America's culturally dominant holidays means that this consideration of special days is not especially diverse. The religion that is most prominent among the culturally dominant holidays is Christianity, simply because the vast majority of Americans identify themselves as Christian, even with the increasing pluralism of American society. In addition, a great variety of specifically ethnic celebrations are not discussed here. Yet, given the parameters that come with this choice of five holidays, I hope that the resulting discussion is not excessively narrow and shows awareness of a larger context. Included along the way are at least brief considerations of Passover, the religions of ancient Rome, Celtic practices, the Mexican Day of the Dead, American civil religion, and more.

My purpose in writing about these five holidays is to distill academically reliable information from a wide range of sources and to provide a candid, straightforward thumbnail history of how each arose and developed. Although we all know some bits and pieces, I hope that these narratives will help readers get a sense of the overall story of each holiday. In addition it is fun to pick up interesting bits of trivia to share with friends or to be the expert at the next holiday party. Further, all the stories together prompt us to reflect more generally on why it is important to have special days in an annual ritual calendar, what purposes they serve, and why they are often so contentious. To contribute to that last goal, in addition to my attempts to distill information, I have come up with two key theoretical frameworks to help us understand these holidays.

Studying the history and development of these five holidays, and various controversies surrounding them, one cannot help but notice some striking similarities among the five. Over time, two summaries of holiday patterns have become very helpful for me, one borrowed and revised, and one of my own creation. They provide overarching interpretive frameworks that will appear several times in the following chapters, and it would be useful to introduce them here.

The first pattern is suggested by Amitai Etzioni, a noted sociologist who has shown considerable interest in holidays and rituals. Reflecting on the societal roles that holidays play, he divides them into two kinds: *recommitment* holidays and *tension management* holidays. As the name suggests, the first kind fosters the recommitment of individuals and groups to their religion or nation or society, socializing and integrating people by reinforcing commitment to shared beliefs and practices. Obvious examples might include Easter for Christians, Passover for Jews, and Memorial Day for United States citizens. In these examples, part of each celebration fosters a recommitment of some kind.

When I mention the other category, tension management, many persons first think of special days when they can relax with a day or weekend off of work, taking time to "mellow out." That indeed may be one way to relieve tension, although it is my observation that relaxation seldom happens on major holidays. We participants frequently talk about the need to recover after a holiday period is over, because we have been exhausted by hectic, complicated schedules, preparations, and events.

Etzioni, however, is thinking about a different kind of tension management, more like unrestrained partying. When a person works hard during the week and parties hard on weekends, or when college students take spring break trips to Florida in the middle of a semester, that might be considered tension management, a kind of release. Beyond such examples for individuals, Etzioni focuses on the role of holidays for a society (he is, after all, a sociologist), and he indirectly suggests that rigid adherence to a society's beliefs and standards might be oppressive and lead to social rebellion without some occasions when "mores that are upheld during the rest of the year are suspended to allow for indulgence."[4] In other words, if societies provide some limited opportunities to let go, members may be more willing to follow social norms the rest of the time. Etzioni's examples of this kind of tension management include New Year's Eve, Mardi Gras, Purim, and Oktoberfest. I would add St. Patrick's Day as it has developed in the United States.

Etzioni acknowledges that some holidays may cross over or combine these two categories, recommitment and tension management, but he believes that most holidays emphasize one or the other. Because of the mixtures, which I see as very common, I think that it might be more helpful, instead of categorizing two *kinds* of holidays, to refer to different *functions* that holidays serve for their participants. I am aware that in the process, I am shifting the focus away from social roles to consider the ways that holidays function both for individuals and for societies. As a further revision, it might be helpful to divide tension management into two separate functions, relaxation and unrestrained behavior. Thus, in a reformulation of Etzioni's helpful categories, I propose considering three *functions* that holidays serve: recommitment, relaxation, and release. *Recommitment* reinforces commitment to shared beliefs and practices; *relaxation* refers to one aspect of tension management, rest and recuperation; and *release* refers to the other aspect, revelry with reduced inhibitions. Viewed in this way, a holiday may strongly embody one function, or it may represent a combination of two or three. The functions vary, depending on the holiday, the society, and the individual participant.

In addition, let me propose another pattern, another list of three: three stages of development that describe how these holidays have become what they are today. This list does not apply to all holidays, but I am convinced that it does apply to the five I have chosen to examine here. To put it in the form of an analogy, all five of the holidays in this book are three-layer cakes. The bottom layer is each holiday's background as a *seasonal celebration*. The second layer is a *religious or national overlay*, when a religion (in these examples, usually Christianity) or a national impulse attempts to supplement, co-opt, or transform the meaning of an already existing seasonal celebration. The third layer is *modern popular culture*, which adds its own wrinkles and transformations to the layers that have come before. Thus, three layers:

Modern Popular Culture

Religious or National Overlay

Seasonal Celebration

Seasonal celebrations arise from the understandable human need and desire to respond to times of the year that bring significant transitions or challenges. For example, in regions where winters are especially harsh, who does not feel exhilaration at the first hints of spring, when sprouts push up through the soil and migrating birds return? It makes sense that individuals and societies would want to do *something* to celebrate the arrival of spring, and indeed, that is exactly what human cultures have done, from prehistory and ancient societies down to today. Likewise, after the hard work of a harvest is completed, when storehouses are bursting with grain and selected livestock have been slaughtered to prepare for winter, isn't it natural to want to kick back and party? Admittedly, some natural transitions might also be tinged with fear, or at least the need to adjust to difficult times. This was and is the case with the approach of winter, when the warmth and long daylight of summer give way to darkness and howling, freezing storms.

Seasonal observances preceded each of the five holidays considered in this book. Christmas is rooted in pre-Christian mid-winter festivities that took place in the midst of darkness; Valentine's Day and Easter both arise from spring observances of fertility and new life; Halloween occurs at a time (around November 1) often seen as the end of the light half of the year and the beginning of the dark half; and Thanksgiving is based in part on harvest celebrations or early winter reflections.

Then comes the second layer. When later religions or nations arose, they frequently attempted to build on seasonal observances that already existed and were widely embraced. During the Roman empire, Christians inserted an annual celebration of the birth of Jesus in the middle of three preexisting winter festivals. When Valentine's Day arose as an annual spring celebration of romance almost accidentally associated with a saint's name, some voices belatedly and awkwardly attempted to add rationales of Christian meaning. Easter grew out of the Jewish Passover, which in turn arose from spring observances that reveled in renewed life and fertility. Halloween got its very name when Christians added All Saints' Day to the time of year when Celts already had ceremonies surrounding harvest, death, ancestors, and supernatural spirits, at the end of summer and fall, when darkness began to reign. And the American Thanksgiving, in part based upon gratitude for the harvest, experienced two additional layers of meaning, a national layer and a Christian layer, sometimes fused and sometimes in tension. Some people see Thanksgiving as a national civic holiday for Americans of many religions and backgrounds, and others see it as an occasion to emphasize the United States as a Christian nation.

When considering the third layer, the impact of modern popular culture, the initial response usually is to think of commercialization. Indeed, every one of the five holidays has provided significant opportunities for the sale of products ranging from decorations to gifts to cards to food and more, and it is certainly true that an emphasis on commodities and marketing can alter the very character of a holiday. Yet commercialization is not the only way in which modern popular culture has changed holidays. For example, several began as festivities with limited ethnic or regional roots and then grew successfully into national observances, and it is interesting to explore how and why that occurred. Some holidays that involved adult parties and disorderly behavior experienced national attempts at domestication, efforts to recast or sanitize activities so that they would be appropriate for families and children. And modern popular culture created new symbols for the holidays, such as Santa Claus, adorable Easter bunnies, Ichabod Crane, and the Great Pumpkin.

These three layers vary considerably in the way they exhibit themselves in the five holidays considered in this volume, sometimes in surprising ways. Whatever the variations, recognizing the three layers may help us understand the controversies and dissatisfactions frequently associated with selected holidays. They undergird the historical summaries in the following chapters.

Before turning to the story of each special day, let's pause for a moment to reflect on the term "holiday." (We academics are always defining terms.) The word comes from the Old English "haligdaeg," meaning holy day, referring to a consecrated day or a religious festival, and in some modern applications it still has that meaning. However, as early as the 1400s it began to take on a more secular meaning as well, referring to a day or days off of work. Many Europeans speak of "going on holiday," which is what is termed "taking a vacation" in the United States. In America, many define the term "holiday" as a day free of work, and so they think of nationally declared holidays or religious special days when exemptions from work are granted. When I have asked audiences to name their favorite holidays, I have noticed that some respondents limit their answers to days when they are officially not working. That certainly is the case in many instances, but I believe that our popular use of the term includes more than just "a day on which one is exempt from work" or even "a day of relaxation." If that is the definition, then Valentine's Day, St. Patrick's Day, and Mother's Day are not holidays, but many do call them holidays. Thus I use the term more broadly, to refer to days exempt from work but also to other socially designated special days for festivity. Birthdays and weddings would be private occasions and not socially designated, but this broader definition would include a wide range of religious, national, and ethnic celebrations. I would argue that most of us use the term in that broader sense, and that is the meaning I have in mind when it appears in this volume.

Christmas

Poll after poll indicates that Christmas is America's favorite holiday. That includes me. While I look forward to many different holidays, and I am especially interested in the five considered in this volume, Christmas is the one that is closest to my heart. My most touching family memories are from Christmastime. I find this season's decorations the most beautiful, its music the most uplifting, and its generous spirit most inspiring. The worship services and spiritual meanings move me.

At the same time I often find myself wishing for more. I recall attending a workshop about how to make Christmas more meaningful. We were asked to read a list of statements and select the ones that were true for us. One of the statements said something like, "When the season comes to an end I find myself refreshed and renewed." I had to laugh, because that was so far from my experience. Everything is so hectic, so pressured, and so expensive, I have to recover once Christmas is over. Is it possible to do anything about the downside of a holiday, and to enhance the other aspects?

It seems to me that the first step in wrestling with this problem is to learn about the holiday, how it began and how it developed and changed. It does not do much good to idealize the past and yearn for a golden age that never was. A realistic understanding of the day and the season could give the most helpful starting point for making decisions about how to approach it in the future.

So, I guess that did give me something of an agenda as I approached my study of the history of Christmas and the other holidays, but I hope it was not a heavy-handed one. Motivated more by curiosity rather than by a desire to prove something, I have had fun developing an overall sense of the story of Christmas, stumbling upon all kinds of interesting nuggets along the way. And it is appropriate to start with Christmas, because it provides an excellent illustration of the three-layer cake outlined in the introduction. The other four holidays will provide interesting twists and variations.[1]

WINTER

The first step in understanding Christmas is to recognize how much it is rooted in winter celebrations.

I live in the Upper Midwest, which has dramatic winter weather, but I began really thinking about the severities of winter when I took a group of college students on a trip to Alaska, where we spent much of our time in the little village of Willow, about an hour and a half north of Anchorage, still in the southern half of Alaska. We were there in May, but we heard what it could be like in the middle of winter, with only four hours of daylight a day and temperatures as low as forty degrees below zero—*before* calculating the wind chill. We heard about difficulties surviving winter in little shacks in the woods with no electricity and no running water, and we heard about the struggles some people had with depression, alcoholism, domestic abuse, and suicide, aggravated by winter. I began wondering what it would have been like to live in central or northern Europe in the Middle Ages, probably under similar conditions. Today we have electric lights and thermostats, but we still battle "cabin fever" or SAD, seasonal affective disorder, in the midst of winter. What must it have been like for northern Europeans in those centuries long before modern conveniences? Seen this way, it becomes clear that under some circumstances, winter is difficult to survive. Entering winter is a little like walking into death and hoping that we will come out on the other side.

I began to speculate about what those people in medieval Europe might have done to cope with the difficulties of winter. Here's a great idea: sponsor a big, blowout midwinter party! The logical time to have it would be in the middle of winter, when the days stop getting shorter and are about to grow longer again. That would be in mid to late December. People in a snowbound village could spend half of the winter distracting themselves with the preparations, and then have the party as a break from suffering the cold and the dark. When the party was over, the remainder of winter would be that much shorter. And it is easy to guess what the party would be like. It would be a festival of lights, with candles, and burning logs, and anything else to push back the darkness. It also would feature evergreens, as signs of life when everything else seems to have died, plus other plants that not only stay green but even bear fruit in the middle of winter, like holly or mistletoe. It probably would include gatherings of family and friends for meals and parties, to overcome the isolation of winter. There would be feasts, and drinking, and dancing, and maybe special songs and gifts of some kind.

As it turns out, all over central and northern Europe, early cultures had winter festivities that included almost all of these features. One example was Yule, or Jul, celebrated in the geographical area now called Germany, Scandinavia, and the British Isles. Today people think that the word "Yule" is a synonym for Christmas, but it actually was the name for the pre-Christian winter celebration in that region. Scholars are unsure what the word meant. It might have been "wheel," as in the cycle of seasons, or perhaps "feast" or "sacrifice." The seasonal activities included the slaughter of animals, a lot of drinking, bonfires and candles, and of course the Yule log, ghost stories, and prickly evergreens around windows to keep away evil spirits. An example of a winter festival further south in Europe was the Roman Saturnalia, a late harvest festival varying in length from three to seven days and held between December 17 and 23. The partying was wild and included drunkenness and all kinds of unrestrained activities, but it also featured the candles and fires, greenery, feasting, gifts, and social gatherings that would be expected of a winter party.

Much of what I have just outlined describes Christmas today: outdoor displays of lights, Christmas trees and other evergreen decorations, gatherings of family and friends, feasts, and songs. All are beloved parts of Christmas but they really have nothing to do with a baby in a manger. They are predictable aspects of mid-winter parties that help people cope with winter. This is what is meant when some refer to "the pagan roots of Christmas." "Pagan" was a word used by Christians to refer to something that was non-Christian or pre-Christian, and it is certainly true that Europeans in central and northern Europe had winter festivals before Jesus ever walked the earth. When Christians eventually started celebrating the birth of Jesus in December and then spread their religion into central and northern Europe, they encountered preexisting winter parties and absorbed aspects of these into their Christmas observances. This is an example of the first two layers of the three-layer cake summarized in the introduction. First there were seasonal celebrations, in this case in the middle of winter, and then Christianity came along and added a new layer of meaning to those celebrations.

This combination of two layers sets off an array of very strong and quite contrasting reactions. Some conservative Christians believe that any association with pre-Christian or non-Christian religions and cultural practices will taint Christianity, and thus they urge Christians either to purify Christmas observances of anything "pagan" or to not observe Christmas at all, because it has been too compromised. Some secular voices are amused by the whole situation and lift up the pagan associations to watch Christians squirm. Some modern pagans or neo-pagans, persons who identify with the pre-Christian European religions in their modern forms, joyfully point to the Christian adoption of some of these practices as a validation of the superiority of their nature-based religions. And some Christians just enjoy the holiday and do not see any issue here. My personal approach is different from all of these alternatives.

What I see here is the common humanity of the different groups. All of us, whatever our religion or culture or historical era, have similar needs as human beings to cope with seasonal changes. In the case of winter, I fully understand how the cold and the dark can become oppressive, and so I love driving around to see Christmas lights, and I love the beauty of evergreen decorations and the chance to get together with others. These things lift my spirits in the dead of winter. If I did not live in a culture that already had a winter party, I would start one! All of us share a common human impulse to celebrate and survive, to search for joy and meaning, in the middle of winter.

CHRISTMAS BEGINNINGS

So, winter came first, and then Christmas was added later, but it took a while.

Early Christians did not celebrate Christmas. For the first couple of centuries of early Christianity, there was no annual celebration of the Christ child's nativity at all. This comes as a big surprise to many Christians, because today Christmas and Easter are the two most special days of the Christian year. It was not always that way. Early Christianity was, instead, an Easter-centered religion. The focus was on the death and resurrection of Jesus. The expectation that Jesus Christ would return soon, at any time, and the examples of Christian martyrdom in times of Roman persecution helped accent an emphasis on death and resurrection themes.

As evidence of what was emphasized and what was not, in the early church, compare the emphasis given to Christmas and Easter in the four gospels of the New Testament. Only two of the four give any significant attention to a nativity story. The gospels of Mark and John do not. The Gospel of Mark begins with John the Baptist and the baptism of Jesus, who by that time was already an adult. In other words, Mark's gospel totally skips a birth or Christmas story. The Gospel of John includes an elegant passage declaring that "the Word became flesh and lived among us" (John 1:14), a common scripture text at Christmastime, but John's gospel contains no story of a baby in a manger, no shepherds, and no wise men.[2]

I was well into adulthood before it dawned on me that virtually all of the New Testament readings at Christmastime came from only two of the four gospels, and even then, they told two stories with quite different details. Matthew's account includes the star and the wise men and the escape to Egypt, but no shepherds. Luke's version has the shepherds and the multitude of angels, but no star or wise men. And except for Paul's one comment about Jesus being "born of a woman" (Galatians 4:4), the entire New Testament, all twenty-seven books, contains no additional references to the nativity story. Because Christmas has become such a major Christian celebration today, it is difficult for us to step back and realize how little attention the New Testament gives to the birth of Jesus compared with some other subjects. When Christians eventually began an annual nativity observance, they had to bring together the tidbits in Matthew and Luke and then add all sorts of later traditions in order to create a very full story.

In contrast, how many chapters in all four gospels are devoted to the death and resurrection of Jesus? A lot. Paul's letters to early Christians make up much of the Christian New Testament; how much attention does he give to death and resurrection? A lot. Most Christians would agree that these themes are the heart of the gospel message. The New Testament itself is evidence that the early church was Easter centered and that any significant focus on Christmas was a later development.

The eastern church (later to become identified as Eastern Orthodox) began Epiphany observances sometime in the 200s or 300s, on January 6, lifting up many ways that Jesus Christ was made manifest in the world. Epiphany means "showing forth," and the day highlighted many ways that people in the world became aware of how extraordinary Jesus was. Epiphany celebrations variously emphasized Jesus's baptism, public miracles by Jesus early in his ministry (such as turning water into wine at a wedding), and, yes, miracles and events surrounding his birth.[3] There was some attention to the birth story, but it was not the only focus for that day. On the other hand, the western part of the early church, centered in Rome, had no equivalent Epiphany observances. The first extant documentary mention of the western church celebrating Jesus's birth appears in the Philocalian Calendar, also known as the Chronograph of 354. It is a collection of documents, something like an almanac, and some of the included texts may date back to 336. Thus, by either 336 or 354, Christians in Rome were celebrating Jesus's birth on December 25. The practice may have begun somewhat before that, but this document is our earliest surviving evidence.[4]

One reason that Christians took so long to start an annual observance of the nativity of Jesus was the Easter emphasis just mentioned. Another reason is that Christians did not know exactly when Jesus was born. In order to have a birthday party for someone, it would help to know their date of birth, but no New Testament passages and no external evidence clearly indicate the month or day in Jesus's case.. Some attempted calculations claimed that Jesus was born on March 25 or 28, April 19 or 20, May 20, and November 18, with no real consensus. Another reason for the delay is that the early Christians tended not to celebrate birthdays. In their view that was something Romans, not Christians, did. When Christians remembered early martyrs who died for their faith, they celebrated the dates of their deaths, not their births. Even today, saints' days on Catholic and Orthodox calendars are the dates that they died.

Why did Christians eventually add a celebration of Jesus's birth, and why on December 25? We do not have enough evidence for a clear answer. It would be very helpful if we had a letter or a proclamation from a pope or an emperor declaring when and why Christians were going to start an annual celebration of the birth of Jesus, but we have no such document. It is a good guess that theological reasons were at least a factor. After the Roman persecution of Christians stopped and Christianity became a favored religion, Christians had the time and freedom to argue with one another about who understood Jesus properly. A birthday celebration could be very useful in the midst of these arguments, to declare that Jesus was divine from the moment of his birth or even before, not at some later point during his earthly lifetime.

Whatever the theological reasoning or the calendar calculations, one reality is clear. In choosing December 25, the western church settled on a date that was precisely in the middle of three wildly popular existing Roman winter festivals. First was the Saturnalia, the Roman late harvest celebration already mentioned, with a legendary reputation for excessive partying. This took place in the middle of December. A couple of weeks later came the new year's festival Kalends, which lasted for as many as five days, with feasts and additional uninhibited celebrations. "Kalends" is a word that refers to the first day of the month, and the first day of the year was the most important among them. Today's word "calendar" derives from that term. In between Saturnalia and Kalends fell December 25, the winter solstice by calendars of that time. Romans celebrated December 25 as the birthday of Sol Invictus, the Unconquered Sun, a god whose devotion had been merged with worship of the warrior god Mithras. (In an attempt to be clever, some have said that Christians changed the birthday of a sun god to a birthday of God the Son.) All three celebrations pervaded Roman culture, so Christian leaders had to have been aware of them. It cannot have been accidental that Christian leaders chose to place the birthday observance for Jesus in the midst of these three notable Roman celebrations. As for why they did it, we can only guess. Perhaps they wanted to co-opt the popularity of the existing winter parties in order to promote the acceptance of Christianity among more people. Perhaps they disapproved of how wild the parties were and hoped that adding a Christian celebration would tame them. Perhaps they wanted to compete with the Roman religions head on. Maybe it was all three.

Whatever the motivations, Christians gave an overlay of Christian meaning to some preexisting winter festivities. An important implication of this narrative is that when Christians finally initiated an annual celebration of the birth of Jesus, it was *from the very beginning* a combination of winter cultural party and Christian observance. Historian Stephen Nissenbaum offers a very articulate summary of the complicated implications:

> The decision was part of what amounted to a compromise, and a compromise for which the Church paid a high price. Late-December festivities were deeply rooted in popular culture, both in observance of the winter solstice and in celebration of the one brief period of leisure and plenty in the agricultural year. In return for ensuring massive observance of the anniversary of the Savior's birth by assigning it to this resonant date, the Church for its part tacitly agreed to allow the holiday to be celebrated more or less the way it had always been. From the beginning, the Church's hold over Christmas was (and remains still) rather tenuous. There were always people for whom Christmas was a time of pious devotion rather than carnival, but such people were always in the minority. It may not be going too far to say that Christmas has always been an extremely difficult holiday to *Christianize*.[5]

Today, when people complain about what has happened to Christmas and launch campaigns to "Keep Christ in Christmas," there is an underlying desire for Christmas to return to the pure spiritual holiday it once was, before recent developments ruined it. The point is, it never was a purely spiritual holiday. Christians started celebrating the birth of Jesus sometime in the 300s, and from the very first it was a fusion of preexisting winter festivals and Christian themes. The struggle to find a balance between the two has continued ever since.

Once the day was chosen to celebrate the birth of Christ, over several centuries a whole season developed around it. With eastern Christians giving importance to Epiphany on January 6, and western Christians celebrating the nativity on December 25, it was almost as if the two sides negotiated a way to recognize both. If December 25 was to be celebrated as Christ's birthday, then January 6 could mark the arrival of the wise men, when the world became aware of the Christ child. The days in between became known as the Twelve Days of Christmas. Even though some Christians think Christmas is over on December 26, according to the church's calendar, the Twelve Days of Christmas are just starting then.

A season also developed leading up to Christmas: Advent. As we will see in the chapter about Easter, Christians established Easter as a special day years before Christmas got started. The church designated the forty days prior to Easter, not counting Sundays, as Lent, a time of spiritual preparation for the great celebration of the resurrection of Jesus. So when Christmas was placed on the calendar, it seemed like a good idea to have a similar period of spiritual preparation for that special day as well. Eastern Orthodox Christians sometimes refer to it as Christmas Lent or Little Lent, but the most common name for it is Advent, a period of four Sundays prior to Christmas. For the Eastern Orthodox Church, it is a little longer.

SNOWBALL

In its early centuries, Christianity first spread around the Roman empire, in the lands surrounding the Mediterranean Sea. A few centuries later, after

Christians had started their December 25 observance of Christ's birth, Christianity advanced northward throughout much of the European continent, and Christmas came along for the ride. (The term "Christmas," meaning Christ's Mass, referring to a special worship service for the occasion, arose somewhat later among English-speaking peoples, in the Middle Ages.) The further north, the more powerful the winters, and in each new region Christians encountered winter festivals. When that happened, Christianity and Christmas sometimes picked up some of those winter traditions and transformed them for Christian purposes, instead of conquering or replacing them.

At some points in Christian history, this was a conscious strategy. The most frequently cited example is from Pope Gregory I, called Gregory the Great, who established an explicit policy of accommodation with native traditions. On June 1, 601, he wrote a letter to Abbot Mellitus containing a message to be delivered to Archbishop Augustine of Canterbury. This was not the more famous Augustine of Hippo, one of Christianity's most influential theologians, but Augustine of Canterbury was important in his own right. He was a Benedictine monk from Rome who was sent by Gregory to evangelize England and is considered one of the founders of the English church. This letter was further guidance from Pope Gregory about how to proceed. In it Gregory referred to non-Christian religions as devil worship, but he was willing to retain many of their customs while trying to change their inner meaning. Gregory wrote,

> The idol temples of that race should by no means be destroyed, but only the idols in them. Take holy water and sprinkle it in these shrines, build altars and place relics in them. . . . When this people see that their shrines are not destroyed they will be able to banish error from their hearts and be more ready to come to the places they are familiar with, but now recognizing and worshipping the true God. And because they are in the habit of slaughtering much cattle as sacrifices to devils, some solemnity ought to be given them in

exchange for this. So on the day of the dedication or the festivals of the holy martyrs, whose relics are deposited there, let them make themselves huts from the branches of trees around the churches which have been converted out of shrines, and let them celebrate the solemnity with religious feasts. Do not let them sacrifice animals to the devil, but let them slaughter animals for their own food to the praise of God, and let them give thanks to the Giver of all things for His bountiful provision. Thus while some outward rejoicings are preserved, they will be able more easily to share in inward rejoicings. It is doubtless impossible to cut out everything at once from their stubborn minds; just as the man who is attempting to climb to the highest place, rises by steps and degrees and not by leaps.[6]

This letter is quite clear about Gregory's approach, and it helps explain many of the Christmas traditions that have developed over the years. However, it would be a mistake to assume that this was the Christian strategy at all times and in all settings. (See the next chapter about Valentine's Day for an example.)

Not only did Christianity accommodate some native traditions, but Christianity's movement from one region to another also helped spread one culture's traditions to other areas. For me, the most helpful image to represent the process is a snowball. Christmas is like a snowball. I am not thinking of a snowball that is thrown but one that rolls. When you push a snowball through the yard in order to create a snowman or a fort, the growing ball of snow picks up all kinds of things: autumn leaves, a mitten dropped by a child, salt thrown near the sidewalk, and who knows what else. In a similar way, Christmas rolled through Europe and elsewhere throughout the world, picking up winter customs as it went, incorporating them into Christmas celebrations and also spreading certain customs from one region to another. The snowball changed size, shape, and color as it rolled, adding and dropping features over time and distance. Folklorists and anthropologists often struggle to explain the exact origins and timing of various Christmas traditions, but whatever the specific details in each case, I think much of the overall process of development was quite understandable. It was a rolling snowball.

Consider the poinsettia. In this case the snowball began rolling when the Spanish brought Christianity to what is now Mexico, bringing the December 25 Christmas celebration with them. There they encountered a beautiful winter-flowering plant that was native to Mexico and known to the Aztecs. What we usually refer to as the petals of the poinsettia are actually green leaves that turn red when they experience long nights of darkness. Technically, the yellow buds in the center are the flowers. What is significant is that the plant comes to full bloom in December, responding to reduced sunlight, and thus it is an ideal symbol or decoration for winter celebrations. So, on December 25, when Christians remembered the nativity of Jesus, this flower was blooming in Mexico. A touching folktale arose about a little peasant girl who wanted to bring a gift to the Christ child but, in tears, realized that she had nothing beautiful enough to offer. Nevertheless she brought a handful of ordinary weeds to the cradle of the baby Jesus, and in a miracle he turned them into brilliant red flowers. Thus the plants received the name *flores de Nochebuena*, or flowers of the Holy Night.

It so happens that the first United States ambassador to Mexico was an amateur botanist. His name was Dr. Joel Roberts Poinsett, and he was instrumental in bringing cuttings of the plant back to the United States in about 1828. The formal botanical name for the plant is *Euphorbia pulcherima*, but the popular American name, poinsettia, obviously recognizes the ambassador. Poinsettias were widely available in the United States by the late 1800s and became a pervasive American symbol of Christmas in the twentieth century. The poinsettia went from being a plant that grew wild in Mexico to being domesticated and mass produced in the United States, with sales of more than thirty million plants annually. Today, according to the Society of American Florists, Christmas and Hanukkah constitute the number one floral-buying holiday in the United States (more than Mother's Day and Valentine's Day), and of the flowering plants purchased in the Christmas season, about three-fourths are poinsettias.[7]

The poinsettia story thus is an example of the snowball process at work. The Spanish brought Christianity and Christmas to Mexico, where it picked up the native red flower as a Christmas symbol, which then rolled into the United States, where it has flourished as a dominant Christmas symbol that is sometimes copied in other parts of the world. The Christmas tree is another example. Early traditions included various evergreens in winter festivals; in the 1500s, it was Germans who first introduced the *tree* as a Christmas home decoration. The House of Hanover spread the Christmas tree custom into England, especially through the popularity of Queen Victoria and Prince Albert; soon thereafter it was copied in the United States. The spread of December Saint Nicholas observances throughout Europe and his subsequent metamorphosis into Santa Claus in the United States is yet another example of snowballing.

PURITAN IMPACT

Many people assume that by the time Christmas reached the American colonies and the new nation of the United States, almost all Christians embraced it as a generally shared celebration. This assumption has been expressed in recent years when people complain that because of cultural and religious pluralism in today's United States, it is no longer possible to automatically wish everyone a Merry Christmas. Store signs read "Happy Holidays" instead of "Merry Christmas," and choir directors have become careful about including Christmas music in public school winter concerts. Many voices yearn for the "good old days," when citizens of the United States were united in their celebration of Christmas and the whole culture recognized it without question.

Yet that is not the way it was in the colonies and the early nation. Everyone did not celebrate Christmas, and the entire culture did not stop to recognize the holiday. Although the population in those early days included some Jews and others who did not identify with Christianity, the major differences about Christmas in early America were between Christians themselves.

The explanation extends back to the Puritan Revolution in England in the 1600s. During the Protestant Reformation a century earlier, many Protestant groups were concerned that Christmas contained too many Roman Catholic elements. However, through some minor revisions of Christmas practices, most Protestants were content to continue the nativity observances and their accompanying cultural elements. The English Puritans, however, along with Presbyterians in Scotland, disapproved of Christmas altogether. They claimed that it was a Catholic innovation that was not practiced in the early church, and they complained that the winter partying provided too many excuses for licentious behavior. One propaganda piece of the time was Josiah King's *Examination and Tryal of Old Father Christmas* (1678). It described Father Christmas, "of the Town of Superstition, in the County of Idolatry," who was accused of having "from time to time, abused the people of this Commonwealth, drawing and enticing them to Drunkenness, Gluttony, and unlawful Gaming, Wantonness, Uncleanness, Lasciviousness, Cursing, Swearing, abuse of the Creatures, some to one Vice, some to another; all to Idleness."[8] Thus, in 1644 the English Parliament, controlled by Puritans under Oliver Cromwell, declared Christmas a day of penance instead of a feast day, and in 1652 it banned any observance of Christmas, inside or outside of churches. The Puritan Parliament made a point of meeting on Christmas Day from 1644 to 1656, and various Puritan laws mandated that shops and other businesses remain open on Christmas Day. Many in the population did not want to give up their holiday, but Puritans sent town criers through cities and villages shouting "No Christmas! No Christmas!" on Christmas Eve.

Even though Puritan control was short-lived, these actions helped break the Christmas tradition in England, with New Year's Day and Valentine's

Day becoming more important for many people. As one commentator noted, "An entire generation of children had grown up without the delightsome Christmas memories on which adult devotion to the holiday seems to depend. Social processes had subtly altered English folkways to fill the gap where the public celebration of Christmas used to be. . . . England had lost much of the Christmas habit. Think of it as Cromwell's last laugh."[9]

A striking illustration of how far Christmas had fallen in England emerges from an examination of the December issues of *The Times* of London from 1790 to 1835, more than a century after the Puritan Revolution. Cultural historians John Golby and William Purdue report that in twenty of those forty-five years, "*The Times* did not mention Christmas at all." Not once. In the other twenty-five years, any references to Christmas "were extremely brief and uninformative." Golby and Purdue acknowledge that other factors in addition to Puritanism accounted for the decline, including urbanization, changes in agricultural practices, and distaste by the elite for the more boisterous aspects of the celebration.[10] For a variety of reasons, including Puritanism, Christmas declined dramatically in England.

New England was the beachhead for English Puritanism in the American colonies, and Puritan disapproval of Christmas extended to the New World. In 1659 the Massachusetts General Court ordered a five-shilling fine for persons who observed Christmas in any way, although by 1681 the law had been repealed. In general, many of the English-speaking colonists who were dissenters from the Anglican Church in England tended to ignore or at least deemphasize Christmas when they came to the colonies. In terms of denominational groups, that would include Congregationalists (the name for Puritans in the American colonies), Presbyterians (members of the Church of Scotland who settled in the colonies), Quakers, Baptists, and Methodists. For example, in 1758 Presbyterian minister Samuel Davies, who eventually became president of the College of New Jersey (later Princeton University), said, "I do not set apart this day for public worship, as though it had any peculiar sanctity, or we were under any obligations to keep it religiously."[11]

However, other Christians in the colonies came from backgrounds that did not include the Puritan suppression of Christmas. Catholics from several nations, the Dutch Reformed, Lutherans from Scandinavia and Germany, and other small German sects all brought their Christmas traditions with them. The Church of England continued somewhat restrained Christmas observances in spite of the history of Puritan opposition. This meant that Christmas celebrations in the early United States were something of a patchwork, with many variations depending on family, denomination, and region. Some Christians celebrated Christmas, and others did not. Those who wanted to observe Christmas were free to do so, but shops and government offices remained open, and in general, business was carried on as usual. In parts of New England, public schools were open on Christmas Day at least into the 1800s. So, in the colonies and the early nation, the whole culture did not stop for Christmas, and everyone did not celebrate the day. This was not because of the opposition of non-Christians; it was because Christians disagreed with each other about whether Christmas was appropriate and important.

Christmas did not come roaring back to prominence in England until the mid-1800s, partly through the influence of Charles Dickens, Queen Victoria, and Prince Albert. Dickens (1812–1870) is best known for his novella *A Christmas Carol*, and some people believe that through his story he virtually created Christmas. That is overstated, but it is certainly true that Dickens had a key part in the English Christmas revival, and his influence on the ensuing English and American Christmas has been significant. When he wrote *A Christmas Carol* in 1843, the first 6,000 copies of the book sold quickly. He gave dramatic public readings of his story to overflowing crowds and sales of the book soared. It also sold well in the United States, and Dickens made two American tours, one before and another years after writing his famous story. On the second visit, in 1867, he embarked on a three-month tour, presenting his famous dramatic readings of *A Christmas Carol* and drawing crowds the way rock stars do today. In Boston, 10,000 tickets were sold weeks before his appearance, and in New York, 150 people stood in the cold all night long to get tickets.[12]

Today, when we read *A Christmas Carol* or see its adaptation in plays or movies, most of us assume that although it is a fictional story, we are also learning about what an English Christmas was like in that era. Not so. Dickens was not simply telling us about Christmas at that time; he also was trying to revive it, to selectively re-create Christmas. Think about the issue of working on Christmas Day. Today, in the United States, the vast majority of businesses are closed, more than at most other times of the year. Thus when Scrooge only grudgingly allowed his clerk to have Christmas Day off, we judge him as particularly insensitive. But in Dickens's time many businesses remained open on Christmas Day, something that the Puritans had pushed for more than a century earlier. That is revealed in the story itself, if you think about it. At the end of the night, when Scrooge's heart has been changed, he throws open his window and calls to a boy on the street, learns that it is Christmas Day, and asks the boy to go to the poultry shop to buy a turkey. That means, of course, that both Scrooge and the boy knew that the shop was open! Scrooge's earlier preference to work through Christmas Day seems more cruel to us now, with our cultural assumptions, than it would have been to Dickens's contemporaries. In writing his story, Dickens was an advocate in the controversies of his day, encouraging the revival or reinvention of Christmas traditions, persuading businesses to close for the holiday, and promoting acts of kindness and charity as an appropriate focus. This is why he wanted Scrooge to look unsympathetic when he insisted on working on Christmas Day, and that is why he wanted Scrooge to change his heart, because he wanted England to do the same thing.

One other thing that most people do not notice about *A Christmas Carol* is that there is very little explicit religion in the story. The baby Jesus in a

HE HAD BEEN TIM'S BLOOD-HORSE ALL THE WAY FROM CHURCH, AND HAD COME HOME RAMPANT.

Bob Cratchit and Tiny Tim. Wood engraving from a nineteenth-century American edition of Charles Dickens's *A Christmas Carol*.

manger is never mentioned, and other comments about something religious, even in passing, are few. What is included is the strong advocacy of a Christmas spirit, mainly defined as generosity. Sociologist James Barnett called it Dickens's "Carol Philosophy," which "combined religious and secular attitudes toward the celebration into a humanitarian pattern. It excoriated individual selfishness and extolled the virtues of brotherhood, kindness, and generosity at Christmas." At Christmas everyone "should forget self and think of others, especially the poor and the unfortunate."[13] The message was one that both religious and secular participants could endorse.

Other major contributors to the revival of Christmas were Queen Victoria and Prince Albert. Queen Victoria succeeded to the throne in 1837, when she was only eighteen years old, and reigned until 1901. We now call most of the century the Victorian era because of her long reign and considerable influence. She was part of the House of Hanover, a royal family of German background that had ruled in England for about a century and often married other royalty from Germany. When it comes to Christmas this was important, because while England had fallen out of the Christmas habit, Germans had not experienced the Puritan opposition the English had. They had continued their Christmas celebrations, including their Christmas tree tradition. England was enchanted by its young queen, and life became even more exciting when she married the handsome Prince Albert of Saxe-Coburg Gotha in 1840. The public appeal of Victoria might be compared to the more recent fascination with Princess Diana and the even more recent celebrity of Prince William and Catherine (Kate) Middleton, now the Duke and Duchess of Cambridge.

In the very first year of their marriage, Prince Albert brought a Christmas tree into Windsor Castle and "turned the royal family's Christmases into semi-public events."[14] Royalty of the House of Hanover had previously brought Christmas trees into the castle, but now that Queen Victoria and Prince Albert were doing it, people were really paying attention. The family

A BEAUTIFUL REPRESENTATION OF THE CHRISTMAS TREE.

Queen Victoria and Prince Albert celebrating Christmas with their children at Windsor Castle. Wood engraving. First published in the *Illustrated London News*, December 1848.

tree became especially famous when, on December 23, 1848, the *Illustrated London News* published an illustration of Victoria, Albert, their children, and a governess gathered around a Christmas tree that had been placed on a table, with small gifts hanging from the boughs and arrayed at the base of the tree. Here was a perfect family Christmas, a model to emulate. Christmas trees were soon the rage in England. In 1850 a similar illustration was printed in the United States in *Godey's Lady's Book*, although Victoria's tiara and Albert's sash were edited out in that version, to make them look like an all-American family.

Queen Victoria and Prince Albert helped return Christmas to a central place in British culture, and they popularized the Christmas tree both in England and in America, but they also contributed to another important shift, namely, to a family-centered Christmas. A Christmas revolving around children and family has become a modern American assumption, but again, it was not always that way. Most of the evidence about Christmas in the early, medieval, and Reformation eras is about the activities of adults—attending special worship services at the parish church, feasting and drinking at the village tavern, and attending seasonal plays—with very little attention paid to children. Victorians wanted to change that. The Victorian era as a whole sought a moral revival that included an emphasis on the family. As described by historian Asa Briggs, "The domestic ties of the family itself were sung more loudly than at any other period of English history. . . . The home was felt to be the centre of virtues and emotions which could not be found in completed form outside."[15] The family was seen as the basic, essential unit of society, and Victoria and Albert seemed to exemplify this theme, experiencing by almost all accounts a happy marriage and producing nine children. A family-centered Christmas fit well with this Victorian emphasis, and the newspaper illustration of the royal family gathered around a Christmas tree promoted not only the tree but the family focus of the occasion.

Similar forces were at work in the United States. Historian Stephen Nissenbaum has written an important book about this very topic, well summarized in the volume's long title: *The Battle for Christmas: A Social and Cultural History of Christmas that Shows How It Was Transformed from an Unruly Carnival into the Quintessential American Family Holiday.* Nissenbaum describes raucous bands of lower-class youths roving the streets at Christmastime, exhibiting public drunkenness, loud singing, and even looting and extortion, behavior that could be truly frightening and dangerous. Nissenbaum argues that Christmas festivities were redirected to become domestic, child-centered activities in the home as a way to combat or marginalize the carousing in the streets. Other American holidays considered here also occasioned rowdy behavior by young men in the streets. The desire to tame crowds by domesticating a holiday to be more family centered and child friendly is a common theme in the chapters to come.

SANTA CLAUS AND COMMERCIALIZATION

Parallel to its revival in England, Christmas became a more widespread cultural phenomenon in the United States in the middle of the 1800s. The Christmas resurgence in England exerted influence on the United States, but an additional, specifically American contribution was the development of Santa Claus. And that leads directly into the most common complaint about the modern Christmas, commercialization.

The American Santa Claus arose out of earlier traditions surrounding Saint Nicholas, who supposedly lived in the 300s in what is now Turkey. In his case it is difficult to know what is history and what is legend, but there are great stories about Nicholas, whatever their status. It is said that Nicholas of Myra was an only child of prosperous parents, and when he became a bishop he resolved to give away all of his wealth before he died. While walking the streets one evening, Nicholas overheard a poor widowed father talking with his three daughters, telling them, in tears, that because he had no

Saint Nicholas, fourth-century bishop of Myra and patron saint of children and seafarers. Wood engraving, American, nineteenth century. Broadside commissioned by John Pintard for the New York Historical Society.

money to provide dowries for them, they would not be able to marry and probably would be sold into slavery or worse. Nicholas returned at night when the family was sleeping and tossed a bag of gold through an open window, providing a dowry for one daughter. He came by on another night with a second bag. The father was extremely grateful and waited in hiding on future nights to learn the identity of their benefactor, and when he caught Nicholas on his third visit the father wanted to tell everyone about the gifts. Nicholas asked him not to, insisting that all credit should go to God. One amusing variant, by the way, is that Nicholas threw the bags of gold down a chimney and they just happened to drop into stockings that had been hung on the mantle to dry, a detail undoubtedly influenced by later stories about Santa Claus. Many of the legends are about the generosity of Nicholas, and about his care for children and young people, but his reputation also grew as a protector of seafarers, merchants, bankers, and even pawnbrokers. He came to be one of the most popular saints in both the eastern and western church, with many churches named after him and prayers offered to him. His appeal seemed to be similar to that of a guardian angel who watched over and protected many people. The day of his death was supposedly December 6, so that was his day on the ritual calendar honoring the saints. Therefore Saint Nicholas was not really a Christmas figure, but his saint's day was in the few weeks leading up to Christmas, and later developments would pull him right into Christmas Eve.

When the Dutch settled New Amsterdam (later New York), some of the early community leaders believed that Nicholas was especially important to their Dutch ancestors, and they helped create a mythology about him and his historical importance to the city. A series of at least six people then played roles in gradually transforming Saint Nicholas into Santa Claus. John Pintard organized a New York Historical Society that met on December 6 and raised a toast to Nicholas, still pictured as a bishop. Washington Irving (the author of stories about Rip Van Winkle and Sleepy Hollow) wrote tales about

Santa Claus, 1849. Wood engraving after T. C. Boyd from an 1849 edition of Clement C. Moore's 1823 poem *A Visit from St. Nicholas*, the first book-length publication of the poem.

Saint Nicholas that clothed him in knickers instead of a bishop's robe and had him flying through the air in a wagon pulled by a horse. Then Clement Moore wrote the most famous poem in the English language, popularly called "The Night before Christmas," which added a sleigh and reindeer with names, shifted Nicholas from his early December date to Christmas, and had him slide down a chimney. (Most people do not notice this, but in the poem his metamorphosis is not yet complete: Moore's Saint Nick is an elf. Read the poem and you'll find the word "elf" as well as references to a *miniature* sleigh and *tiny* reindeer.) There is a dispute over whether Moore actually wrote the poem, but if he did, all three of these people were New Yorkers and even knew each other. The Dutch name for Saint Nicholas was Sinterklas, which easily became Santa Claus in the midst of these other transitions.

Then came editorial cartoonist Thomas Nast (known for creating the donkey and elephant as symbols for America's two major political parties), who drew iconic pictures of Santa Claus that added elves, the North Pole, and much more to the Santa mythology. It is remarkable that much of the lore about Santa came not from a writer but from Nast's illustrations that were published in *Harper's Weekly* over a span of almost thirty years. Francis Church wrote the famous editorial "Yes, Virginia, there is a Santa Claus," adding to the magic, and department store Santas began to appear. Finally, commercial artist Haddon Sundblom created at least one Coca-Cola Santa painting annually for thirty-three years, helping establish a universally recognized image. If most people drank Coke in the summer when it was hot, it made sense for the company to launch an advertising campaign to promote the drink in the winter, and Santa was the ideal representative, one whose red and white garb just happened to match the brand colors of Coca-Cola. Mention Santa Claus, and the picture that comes to almost everyone's mind is Sundblom's Santa.

All six of these people—Pintard, Irving, Moore, Nast, Church, and Sundblom—were American, and most were from New York, qualifying Santa Claus as a thoroughly American creation.[16] Santa can be evaluated in many

Santa Claus, 1881. Wood engraving after Thomas Nast.

different ways, as a protector, a disciplinarian (are the children naughty or nice?), a gift giver, and a merchandising agent. The public embraced Santa Claus, businesses promoted him, and Christmas became a dominant, nearly universal cultural celebration in the United States.

Through most of the history of Christmas, gifts did not play the dominating role that they do now. When gifts were given they often were tokens, not major investments. In the 1700s and 1800s, industrialization led to the mass production of commodities and the development of a consumer culture, which inevitably had an impact on Christmas. A decisive shift came when businesses recognized the marketing possibilities associated with holidays. The previous business attitude was represented by Scrooge in Dickens's *Christmas Carol*, when he complained that holidays were simply a way of picking his pocket because he had to pay people for no work. From this perspective, holidays were a time of idleness and were not productive. However, if holidays held potential for the sale of additional products, whether food, clothing, decorations, or gifts, businesses not only tolerated holidays but actively promoted them. Gift-giving traditions already existed in association with both Saint Nicholas Day and New Year's Day. In the United States in the 1800s, for reasons we do not yet fully understand, those gift traditions seem to have migrated across the calendar and converged on Christmas. Undoubtedly the morphing of Santa Claus played a role.

The late 1800s also was the time when handmade gifts gave way to manufactured goods. If you want to trace the commodification of the holiday, chart the first appearances of many of the products we now associate with Christmas. You will find that most of them arose in the nineteenth century, with further developments in the twentieth. The first Christmas card appeared in England in 1843, and use of such cards became widespread in the United States in the second half of the century. Christmas trees were sold on the streets of New York as early as 1840; light bulbs for Christmas trees first appeared in the 1880s, and glass ornaments appeared in the 1890s.

Wrapping paper appeared at the end of the nineteenth century and became more colorful in the twentieth. The list goes on and on.

Yet among all the products, gifts certainly have become central to the modern American Christmas. Surveys indicate that 97 percent of Americans buy Christmas presents, and those presents total more than $200 billion annually. One estimate claims that 20 percent of all retail sales in the United States are for Christmas purchases of one kind or another.[17] Consumer spending for the other holidays considered in this book is substantial, but spending on all of them *together* is dwarfed by the amount spent in the Christmas season.

One way to look at all of the developments described here is that there are two Christmases, a Christian Christmas and a cultural Christmas, and they have existed side by side from the beginning. The Christian Christmas, of course, includes the activities focused on the birth of Jesus and its meaning, including worship services, special music, prayers, and devotions. The cultural Christmas is almost everything else, including feasts, parties, gifts, and decorations. All along the way, people could celebrate one or the other or both. Many features can fit into both the cultural and the religious holiday. For example, the great emphasis in Dickens's *Christmas Carol* on the Christmas spirit of generosity toward the less fortunate certainly can be seen emblematic of Christian love, but people who do not view themselves as Christians also can be inspired to engage in such generosity at Christmastime.

An interesting example is what is now happening in Japan. According to Japanese international students at my college and friends who are Japanese or who have lived there, in the Christmas season about half of Japanese homes display artificial Christmas trees decorated with lights, origami, and fans, shopping areas have seasonal decorations, and gifts are exchanged. Yet only about two percent of the Japanese population is Christian. One friend tells me most people know that Christmas, or Kurisimasu, has something to do with the birth of Jesus, but for them it is mostly a time for decorations and the exchange of gifts with no special religious meaning. These customs may have been introduced by American occupation forces following World War II, or they may have been appealing because the west seemed exotic, or they may have taken root because so many products for the American Christmas market were produced in Japan. Whatever the reasons, the Japanese clearly are celebrating a cultural Christmas. Should Christians be angry that the Japanese have these customs; should they insist that people engage in Christmas activities only if they always keep Jesus in mind? Or is it acceptable for persons to be drawn to the cultural Christmas even if they have other religious interests or none at all?

The same situation obviously exists in the United States as well. Some of the conflicts about Christmas in American culture arise from the fact that some people observe a Christian Christmas, some a cultural Christmas, and many combine both. In a similar way, can the three functions of holidays apply here? Some persons see Christmas primarily as a time for recommitment, some enjoy it as a time of release, some find time for relaxation, and many exhibit combinations of these functions.

Finally, Christmas offers a clear example of the three-layer cake described in the introductory chapter. Much of what is now identified as belonging to Christmas is rooted in the predictable and understandable features of winter parties: lights, evergreens, feasts, and social gatherings, maybe music and gifts as well. This kind of holiday is a way to survive winter. The second layer was added when Christianity arose and chose to place the celebration of the birth of Christ in the middle of existing winter parties, adding a new layer of Christian meaning. The third layer, added by modern popular culture, has superimposed many new symbols and twists, including the transformation of Saint Nicholas into Santa Claus, the rise of extravagant gift giving and its vital role in the American economy, and the emphasis on both family and generosity in the Victorian era and thereafter.

Valentine's Day

"Keep the 'Saint' in St. Valentine's Day!" is the name of one of Facebook's affinity groups. The title is whimsical, of course, playing on the familiar slogan about keeping Christ in Christmas. Yet it also raises questions. For most of my life, whenever I have participated in the Valentine's Day ritual of giving cards, candy, and flowers to loved ones, I have seldom paused to think about the name or the history of the day. I suspect

Illustration of a valentine, wood engraving, 1854.

I am not alone in that. Yet once in a while something brings to the surface questions lurking in the back of my mind. Who was Saint Valentine, anyway? Does Valentine's Day have anything to do with religion at all? How did the day become associated with romance, hearts, Cupid, greeting cards, and candy? Is this just a holiday trumped up by Hallmark?

First, how did it all begin?

A DOUBTFUL HISTORY

The conventional history of the origin of Valentine's Day, repeated in many books and on many websites, is a story of Pope Gelasius I suppressing a wild Roman festival and replacing it with the celebration of Saint Valentine, a Christian martyr. Briefly, the three-part story goes like this.

1. The Lupercalia was an annual mid-February Roman party involving purification and fertility rites. Men drew the names of women out of a box, to be their consorts for the next year, and nearly naked young men ran through the streets waving bloody strips of leather in the air, to promote women's fertility and to ease the pain of childbirth.

2. In the 200s, in the era of Roman persecution of Christians, a priest named Valentine (or perhaps a bishop, or perhaps there were two different people) was beheaded for refusing to deny his faith. One legend indicated that Valentine had performed underground weddings for romantic couples when the Roman emperor had banned them. Another told of Valentine healing his jailor's blind daughter. Yet another story recounted how Valentine fell in love with this same daughter and just before his execution wrote her a note expressing his affection, signed "From your Valentine."

3. Two centuries later, in 495, after the Roman persecution of Christians had ended and Christianity had become the religion of

the empire, Pope Gelasius I banned the Lupercalia because it was too licentious, and he placed the commemoration of Saint Valentine in its place, on February 14, encouraging more appropriate Christian romantic relationships.

This narrative, with the drama of persecution, and healing, and romance, and underground weddings, and a love note, is appealing. It also serves as a perfect illustration of the first two layers of the three-layer cake outlined in the introduction, with a Roman pre-Christian spring fertility festival (layer one) transformed into a Christian celebration of love and relationships (layer two).

If only it were true.

The problem is, throughout the next eight or nine hundred years, there is no substantial evidence of romantic couples in Europe doing anything special annually on or around February 14. If this really was the beginning of Valentine's Day, would you not expect something to have begun?

In the view of a number of scholars, a stronger case can be made for the late Middle Ages as the period when Valentine's Day arose as a romantic occasion, and I will explain that shortly. First, examining the conventional story, what is historically verifiable and what is not?

Ancient Rome did indeed have an annual Lupercalia observance in the middle of February, on February 15. One description comes from Plutarch (c. AD 45–120), the Greek historian and essayist who became a Roman citizen and wrote numerous biographies of Roman emperors and other famous figures. In his *Life of Romulus* Plutarch admitted that he was not exactly sure of the Lupercalia's origins and significance. It involved the story of the founding of Rome, with Romulus, Remus, and the she-wolf, but it was also a rite of purification and fertility. However, Plutarch was clear in describing the activity:

> The priests slaughter goats, and then, after two youths of noble birth have been brought to them, some of them touch their foreheads with a bloody knife, and others wipe the stain off at once with wool dipped in milk. The

youths must laugh after their foreheads are wiped. After this they cut the goats' skins into strips and run about, with nothing on but a girdle, striking all who meet them with the thongs, and young married women do not try to avoid their blows, fancying that they promote conception and easy child-birth. A peculiarity of the festival is that the Luperci [priests] sacrifice a dog also.[1]

The Roman poet Ovid, the Roman scholar Varro, and the Christian theologian Augustine all discussed or mentioned the Lupercalia, but the festivity probably is most remembered today because, in 44 BC, Mark Antony became one of the Lupercalia runners and took the occasion to offer a crown to Julius Caesar. Shakespeare later referred to this incident in his tragedy *Antony and Cleopatra*. Overall, numerous historical indications verify that the Lupercalia existed as a Roman observance, but with a major caveat: although there probably was wild partying, there is no reliable evidence that it involved a ritualized time when men drew the names of women, or that it involved the pairing of lovers. That claim came much later, as a creative addition, after the emergence of a romantic Valentine's Day.

What about Saint Valentine? The background for Valentine's story is the persecution of Christians in the Roman empire in Christianity's first two or three centuries. The persecution was not constant, instead varying with the inclinations of emperors and local rulers, and it ended when the Edict of Milan in AD 313 finally granted toleration for Christians. In the earlier centuries Roman authorities sometimes blamed Christians for undermining the empire's unity by refusing to acknowledge Roman gods, and the penalty could include death by crucifixion, stoning, fire, wild animals, or decapitation. A number of Christians saw the threats as a test of faith and chose to die rather than deny their Lord. Those who died were called martyrs, and a cult of martyrdom developed, with elaborate narratives about their courage, collections of their bones as relics, and prayers to martyrs as intercessors with God. The admiration of martyrs evolved into a broader veneration of "saints,"

Ualentinus

Saint Valentine, late-third-century Christian martyr. Woodcut from the
Nuremberg Chronicle, German, 1493.

exemplars of faith, and the dates of their deaths became part of an annual calendar for the Christian church as a focus for prayer and inspiration. (As mentioned in the Christmas chapter, note that it was not the dates of their births that were remembered but rather the dates of their deaths.) The early Christian theologian Tertullian remarked that "the blood of the martyrs is the seed of the church," indicating how important martyrdom became for the inspiration and growth of early Christianity.[2]

Valentine was one of those martyrs, but there may have been more than one. Valentine was a popular name in the Roman empire, apparently derived from the Latin "valeo," meaning "be strong." Scholar Jack Oruch notes that "several emperors and a pope bore the name, and more than thirty Valentines and a few Valentinas achieved sainthood, primarily through martyrdom."[3] We know very little about most of them, but two became the center of attention: a priest in Rome and a bishop of Terni, both supposedly beheaded on February 14, with suggested years of 269, 270, or 273, and buried within sixty miles of each other on the Flaminian Way.

The *priest* Valentine, of Rome, is said to have been arrested under the Emperor Claudius. Called before the emperor, Valentine defended his faith and was confined to the household of a nobleman, Asterius. Some accounts refer to Asterius as Valentine's jailor, but it sounds more as if Valentine were under house arrest. Valentine healed the sight of the nobleman's adopted daughter, blind from cataracts since age two, which prompted Asterius and his entire household of forty-four to convert to Christianity. When Claudius learned of the healing and the conversions, he had Valentine beheaded, and Asterius was sent away to be tried and executed.

The *bishop* Valentine, of Terni, encountered a scholar named Crato who asked Valentine to heal his son, "crippled since the age of three by a disease that contorts his body, forcing his head between his knees and depriving him of speech."[4] Valentine attempted to convert Crato, saying that only the father's faith could cure the boy. When Crato was unable to make a commitment,

Valentine agreed to heal the son through Valentine's own faith, expecting Crato and his household to convert if the healing was successful. Valentine locked himself in a room with the boy, and eventually both their voices were heard singing. Crato, his household, affiliated Greek scholars, and many others converted to Christianity. When Roman senators heard the news, they had Valentine beaten and beheaded. Crato and the scholars were arrested and executed.

These stories sound quite similar to each other, with both Valentines defending the Christian faith before authorities, healing children, and causing conversions of households, leading to the beheading of both on February 14 and the execution of the persons Valentine converted. Is it any wonder that scholars have asked if the two accounts are connected? Perhaps it started as a single narrative about one person, but as details changed in the transmission of the story, it developed into two separate versions. Or perhaps there were two Valentines, with information about one and almost no information about the other, and details from one were borrowed to apply to the second Valentine. Other possibilities? At this distance it is difficult to solve the mystery.

There are some other problems. The admiring stories (hagiographies) of martyrs like these are called "acts" or "passions," and the earliest surviving tales about Valentine were written in the 500s or 600s, considerably after the lifetime of either Valentine. The narratives were part of a literary genre that freely mixed history and legend, not in an attempt to be dishonest (because history had different standards then than it does now), but to glorify those who were heroes in the faith. One difficulty concerns Claudius, the emperor who supposedly arrested the priest Valentine. No persecutions took place during the rule of the first Claudius, so some historians have suggested it must have been Claudius II. Yet the evidence is slim there as well, because Claudius II had a very short reign (March 268 to April 270) and spent almost all of his time outside of Italy in military ventures. His predecessor had a policy of toleration, and there is little direct evidence that Claudius II changed it. Another historical difficulty is that one of the earliest lists of martyrs (the Philocalian Calendar, also known as the Chronograph of 354) does not include Valentine. On the other hand, there is evidence that by the mid-300s, some traditions had begun forming around both the priest and the bishop in certain localities in Italy. That evidence includes the building of churches with Valentine's name, claims of relics, and some archaeological fragments. We simply do not know what is historical and what is legend in the traditions.

By the early 700s, the Venerable Bede, an English monk and scholar often referred to as the Father of English History, knew of the accounts of both Valentines and included abstracts of their stories in his list of martyrs. His accounts of both were repeated widely thereafter. However, in 1969 the influential worldwide Roman Catholic council Vatican II revised the calendar of saints, and several saints were removed from the General Roman Calendar. One was Valentine. (Another, by the way, was Saint Nicholas.) Days in their honor were not totally eliminated, but they were reduced to optional special days in particular localities. Regarding Valentine, the reason was simply that very little historical information about him could be verified.[5]

Whatever the historical difficulties, something else very important is missing from this discussion of Saint Valentine: there are no stories about romance. The early traditions, the hagiographies of the 500s and 600s, and the summaries by Bede do not include any claims that either one of the two Valentines performed underground weddings, or fell in love with the nobleman's daughter, or wrote a love note "from your Valentine." Again, these are creative additions that were added later. No disrespect intended, but without those later additions, the one or two Valentines are almost indistinguishable from many other martyrs of the period; they died courageously rather than renounce their Christian faith, and they were credited with miraculous healing. Nothing more, nothing less. No romantic connections.

The final piece in the conventional history of Valentine's Day is Pope Gelasius I. He indeed served as bishop of Rome, or pope, from 492 until his death in 496, in an era when persecutions of Christians were long past. In the early 300s Constantine had become the first Roman emperor to accept Christianity, and Christianity thereafter was tolerated in the Roman empire, then favored, and eventually became the official state religion. Now the church was in control, and Gelasius, although his papal term was brief, was a vigorous advocate for the authority and prerogatives of the church. One example was his stand against the Lupercalia.

It is unclear why the Lupercalia was still being celebrated, because previous popes already had suppressed almost all of the major pagan (pre-Christian or non-Christian) Roman religious celebrations. Apparently the Lupercalia had declined, but its observance hung on tenaciously and then experienced something of a revival, becoming more of a general cultural practice involving not just the nobility but the average population, including Christians. When Gelasius (or possibly his papal predecessor Felix III) insisted that Christians should not participate in the Lupercalia, he met resistance from some Roman senators. Gelasius then wrote a long letter—really a full argumentative treatise—making his case to Andromachus and other Roman senators. In the letter Gelasius reviewed his understanding of the history and purposes of the Lupercalia, and this letter is one of the sources historians consult today when trying to understand the nature and development of the Roman rite.

Senators charged that the suppression of the Lupercalia had caused disease and adversity for Rome, but Gelasius scoffed at their claim, answering that such difficulties had also happened earlier, when the Lupercalia was still being celebrated. He added that even the Lupercalia's advocates should be ashamed of what it had become, because it was allowed "to be celebrated carelessly, and with much less reverence and piety than your ancestors in paganism celebrated it."[6] More important, Gelasius argued that the Lupercalia involved vile songs, jesting and personal humiliation, general immorality and licentiousness, and the worship of demons, and he declared "that no one baptized, no Christian, should be defiled by the pagan rites."[7]

However, as with the other portions of the conventional Valentine history considered thus far, a very significant piece is missing. There is no indication that in suppressing the Lupercalia, Gelasius put anything else in its place. Much later, in the 1500s, a Cardinal Baronius speculated that Gelasius converted the Lupercalia into the Feast of the Purification of the Virgin (or Candlemas), changing one purification ceremony into another, and many noted authors have repeated the claim. Recent scholarship has refuted Baronius's assertion, although the details, involving chronological developments and dates that do not fit, are a bit complicated to explain here.[8]

More important for this story, there is no evidence that Gelasius advocated a celebration of Valentine's Day as a replacement for the Lupercalia. It is a coincidence that at the time the February 15 Lupercalia was suppressed, the Christian calendar of martyrs had already begun including an adjacent date, February 14, in the name of Valentine. It is just that, a coincidence, with no indication of a connection. The letter by Gelasius to Andromachus criticizing the Lupercalia contains no reference to Valentine, or Valentine's Day, or any replacement observance.

In some other cases, Christians did try to co-opt non-Christian festivals, transforming them into occasions with Christian meaning; Christmas is one example. Valentine's Day is not. As scholar Jack Oruch summarizes the letter from Pope Gelasius to Andromachus, "At no point does Gelasius speak of compromise or of adapting any pagan customs: Christians must not keep a place in their hearts for a superstition incompatible with their faith, nor should they contaminate the dignity of their religion and the sanctity of the church. Obstinate violators are to be excommunicated."[9] Pope Gelasius believed that the Lupercalia was anti-Christian, and he wanted it eliminated. No compromise, no transformation. He did not create a new holiday in its place.

Thus, the conventional version of the beginnings of Valentine's Day contains *pieces* of verifiable history. However, the pieces do not fit together to provide an adequate explanation of the beginning of a romantic Valentine's Day unless later imaginative additions and speculative connections are added. For almost a thousand years following the lifetime of Gelasius, we have no evidence of a tradition of activities for romantic couples on February 14. The origin must lie elsewhere.

CHAUCER AND COURTLY LOVE

So, when did Valentine's Day really begin? The prevailing theory at the moment is that it arose in the late Middle Ages, through the poetry of a circle of friends, most notably Chaucer. Yes, that is the Chaucer famous for *The Canterbury Tales*, written in the Middle English that drives today's high school and college students crazy. However, Chaucer's innovation arose out of medieval traditions about courtly love, and we should begin there.

Most of us have heard of "courtly love," which conjures images of a chivalrous knight who falls in love with a faraway queen or princess he might never meet in person. He expresses his love and devotion in letters and poems and wears the colors of his lady into battle, although in most cases he knows that her virtue makes any physical sexual fulfillment between them impossible. These themes are widely recognized today because they appear in medieval and later accounts of Arthurian legends (King Arthur, Queen Guinevere, and Lancelot), in popular medieval histories such as Barbara Tuchman's *A Distant Mirror*, and in movies and other forms of popular culture.

Although the phrase "courtly love" was not coined and defined until the 1800s, and much of the literature is romanticized and idealized beyond historical realities, there was some substance to it. It makes sense that in medieval times, when marriages among royal families were arranged more for diplomatic purposes than for the sake of loving relationships, participants might seek an outlet to express feelings of love or attraction not found in marriage. This courtly love was supposed to be both passionate and spiritual. While it gave expression to the erotic desire and intense devotion that might be absent in an arranged marriage, its focus was to be on the uniting of two souls more than on any kind of physical fulfillment.

Attempts to trace medieval courtly love traditions in history usually point to the period of the First Crusade (1096–1099) and thereafter, when nobility and other knightly warriors were away from their families for long periods of time. Courtly love traditions arose in France and England and spread elsewhere in Europe, disseminated by troubadours, poets, and legendary stories.

One of the classic books that helped codify the tradition was *De Amore* by Andreas Capellanus (Andrew the Chaplain), apparently a twelfth-century chaplain to a French court. The title of his book has been translated into English as *About Love*, or more frequently as *The Art of Courtly Love*. Capellanus indicated that he wrote it for his friend Walter, to educate him in the ways of love and women. One of the sections quoted most often is a list of his "rules of love," including the following examples:

> Marriage is no real excuse for not loving.
> It is well known that love is always increasing or decreasing.
> No one should be deprived of love without the very best of reasons.
> When made public love rarely endures.
> The easy attainment of love makes it of little value; difficulty of attainment makes it prized.
> Jealousy, and therefore love, are increased when one suspects his beloved.
> When a lover suddenly catches sight of his beloved his heart palpitates.
> Nothing forbids one woman being loved by two men or one man by two women.[10]

It is provocative even today to consider the rules one by one and see what discussions arise.

Manuscript illumination from *Romance of the Rose*, France, 1487–1495.

Another classic book was the lengthy thirteenth-century French poem *Roman de la Rose (Romance of the Rose)*, an allegory about love written by Guillaume de Lorris and extended by Jean de Meun. As one literature professor has written, "Anyone who wants to know what everybody read from the twelfth to the fifteenth centuries might well peruse *The Romance of the Rose . . .* [which is] called the book most characteristic of the Middle Ages."[11] As might be expected of a work by more than one author, altered over time, the views of courtly love expressed in it vary considerably, from romantic to cynical, but the poem was immensely popular and widely influential.

Whether the patterns of courtly love promoted by *The Romance of the Rose* and *About Love* actually existed in medieval history is, in a way, beside the point. What is clear is that the books were part of a literary and cultural courtly love tradition that circulated among the nobility and the educated, whether the aristocracy really enacted it in their lives or not.

Into this context came Geoffrey Chaucer (c. 1343–1400), generally acknowledged as the Father of English Literature because he helped develop and bring respectability to vernacular English at a time when French and Latin dominated literary work even in England. It is fitting that he was the first writer to be laid to rest in what is now called Poet's Corner in London's Westminster Abbey. Among the many aspects of his literary legacy, he stood in the courtly love tradition, building upon and sometimes critiquing predecessors of the previous two or three centuries.

The examples are many. Chaucer certainly was familiar with *The Romance of the Rose*, because he translated the entire work into English. His famous *Canterbury Tales* includes sections that exemplify courtly love (The Knight's Tale) and other sections that question or satirize it (for example, The Wife of Bath's Tale). Chaucer's *Troilus and Criseyde* borrows an ancient Greek story about the Trojan War and portrays Troilus as an example of a courtly lover. Chaucer also composed love poetry for the court of Richard II, his patron. C. S. Lewis, widely known for his Christian writings but also a noted specialist in medieval studies, called Chaucer the "poet of courtly love" who wrote "for a scholastic and aristocratic age."[12] Another scholar has commented, "The fact that Chaucer is a love poet, the first of any consequence in English and one of the finest who ever wrote, would seem too obvious to be worth mentioning were it not for the scant recognition it receives today."[13] And it was Chaucer as love poet who seems to have written the first poems that brought together references to Valentine's Day, love, and the mating of birds.

Most attention has been given to a lengthy poem called *The Parliament of Fowls*, written sometime in the 1370s or 1380s. Specialists disagree about the exact date and occasion for the poem, but some argue that it was written for Richard II in the midst of his marriage negotiations with either Princess Marie of France or Anne of Bohemia. Briefly, the narrator in the poem tells of a dream or vision he has in which he enters a beautiful sunlit garden and sees a queen, Nature (called Dame Nature or goddess Nature in some modernized translations) sitting on a flowery hill, with birds of every imaginable kind gathered around. The key lines are 309-310, where the narrator says, in Middle English:

> For this was on seynt Valentynes day,
> Whan euery bryd comyth there to chese his make[14]

Or, in modern English,

> For this was on Saint Valentine's Day,
> When every bird comes there to choose his mate

Valentine's Day is then mentioned three more times in the poem, emphasizing that this was an annual occurrence. In lines 320-322, referring to Nature, we have the following:

> So this noble Empress, full of grace,
> Bade every fowl to take its proper place
> As they were wont to do from year to year,
> On Saint Valentine's Day, standing there.[15]

Lines 386-392 again refer to Saint Valentine's Day as a day for birds to choose their mates, and the final Valentine remark welcomes the approach of summer, indicating that this gathering of birds was a spring occasion (lines 680-684).

This poem raises some obvious questions. First, was there a long-standing traditional belief before Chaucer's time that birds chose their mates on February 14, also called Valentine's Day? So far, scholars have not found earlier indications of such a link. If Chaucer was, in essence, inventing a tradition, that may be the reason he repeated the point more than once. On the basis of this poem and other considerations, two scholars, working independently, argued in the 1980s that Chaucer was the originator of Valentine's Day as a day of mating or romance. Jack B. Oruch, a specialist in medieval and early modern literature at the University of Kansas, concluded that Chaucer was "the original mythmaker in this instance," and Henry Ansgar Kelly, director of UCLA's Center for Medieval and Renaissance Studies, agreed that "it was Chaucer who introduced St. Valentine's Day to the world as a mating festival."[16] Both were properly cautious in making their claims and were open to alternative theories, but their perspective has not yet been supplanted. In spite of these academic contributions, conventional histories are tenacious and have a life of their own, and the origin story about the Lupercalia, Valentine, and Pope Gelasius continues to circulate widely.

A second question: Isn't February 14 a little early for a spring ritual? Obviously, geographical location would make a difference in the answer. That factor aside, Oruch and Kelly have two interesting, quite different explanations. Oruch thinks that February 14 is not too early and can indeed be considered at least as the *beginning* of spring. He maintains that European calendars in Chaucer's time, and before Chaucer, had birds singing, and early flowers blooming, and farming preparations (such as grafting) beginning in mid-February. Oruch also argues that love in Chaucer's poems involves tensions between sadness and joy, and that "the alternating warm and cold weather of early spring does form a parallel with the experience of the lovers in his Valentine poems."[17] On the other hand, Kelly is convinced that Chaucer's Valentine references assume a late spring. He notes that of the several Valentines who became saints, one was Valentine of Genoa, whose death was observed on May 3, and Kelly develops a detailed case that Chaucer had Valentine of Genoa in mind when he wrote his poems. If Kelly is right, then May 3 is the date Chaucer intended to serve as a symbol for spring, and it certainly would be a more typical spring day. The shift from one Valentine's date to another, May 3 to February 14, Kelly suggests, resulted from confusion on the part of Chaucer's literary imitators about the two saints with the same name.[18]

A third question is somewhat related to the others. *Why* did Chaucer choose to associate nature, love, and romance with Valentine's Day? To be honest, it is anyone's guess. However, if the arguments of either Oruch or Kelly, or both, make sense, it appears that Chaucer's references to Valentine's Day are intended to be a symbol for the time of year—spring—and have virtually nothing to do with any aspect of Saint Valentine's life. Instead of referring to a specific calendar date, February 14 or May 3, wouldn't it be more poetic to identify a day by utilizing the name of a saint remembered in that general time period? The words "Valentine's Day" have a poetic ring. The words "February 14" do not. Thus, when Chaucer referred to Valentine's Day, it is likely that he was not drawing upon anything significant about the saint but was just borrowing a poetic name to designate a special spring day.

Mention of Valentine's Day appears not only in *The Parliament of Fowls* but also in other writings by Chaucer. In addition, Valentine references and developed themes appear in poetry by several of Chaucer's contemporaries and friends whose names are now less familiar to most of us: Oton de Granson (or Grandson), John Gower, and Sir John Clanvowe, and a few years later, Christine de Pizan and Charles d'Orleans. A tradition was forming.

In the same era, John Lydgate (c. 1370–c. 1451), a monk and poet who admired Chaucer's work and was a friend of Chaucer's son, may have been the first person to use the term "valentine" not only to refer to the saint or day but also to designate a type of poem.[19] Lydgate's innovation highlights an important shift. Think about it. Today when we use the term we're not always referring to the historical or legendary saint or to the day:

"I wrote a valentine for my love" refers to a *poem or letter.*

"I sent a valentine" in more modern days often refers to a *card.*

"Be my valentine" refers to a *person* of our affection.

As early as John Lydgate, the word "valentine" was being used in multiple senses, and the variety of usages continues today.

One might wonder why the writing of a few lines in poems such as Chaucer's *Parliament of Fowls* would be influential enough to start an annual Valentine's Day romantic tradition. Part of the answer is that the poems were connected to an already established literary tradition about courtly love, one that reached back several centuries. However, the courtly love themes had not been associated with any particular date or time of year; they were applicable to life year-round. Chaucer's innovation—associating nature, spring, lovebirds, and romance with Valentine's Day—provided a specific date for a focused celebration of the themes of love. Passionate and spiritual love now had a place, a special day, on the annual ritual calendar. That was the innovation of Chaucer and his poet friends.

The context of courtly love is important for another reason, suggested in part of the name itself, *courtly.* This literary tradition, in which Chaucer participated, was for and about the nobility. In its beginnings, Valentine's Day was mainly for the aristocracy, not the average person. Other social classes began to celebrate it later.

Trying to identify the "first" of anything is something of a game, but Charles d'Orléans (Charles, Duke of Orléans) is commonly recognized as the author of the first valentine in any language—in other words, the first person to send a love poem or letter to a loved one for Valentine's Day. Charles (1395–1465) was a member of the French royal family during the Hundred Years' War, when England was attempting to lay claim to French regions. Charles was captured by the English at the Battle of Agincourt in 1415 and spent the next quarter of a century in England. He was briefly imprisoned in the Tower of London but spent most of the time under house arrest in various castles of the English nobility. (There is a connection here with Joan of Arc, because one of Joan's intentions when she led the French into battle was to free Charles from English control. She did not succeed.)

Charles was himself a poet, and in 1416, a year after his capture, he wrote a little poem in French (not English) to his second wife, Bonne d'Armagnac. In it Charles indicates that he regrets being separated from her for a whole year, repeating the refrain "I am already sick from love, my very gentle valentine." The fact that he was influenced by the poetry of Chaucer and his poetic circle cannot be doubted; Charles read their works while in captivity. (Also, one of the noblemen who kept Charles in his castle, William de la Pole, was married to Chaucer's granddaughter.)

For the oldest English-language love letter associated with Valentine's Day, most people point to a letter written in February 1477 by a woman named Margery Brews to John Paston of Norfolk, England. The couple was considering marriage but their parents were wrestling over the issue of a dowry. The letter was written in Middle English, similar to the language of Chaucer's *Canterbury Tales*. If we render the letter in a modernized form, Margery addressed it to "my right well-beloved Valentine," commending herself to John "full-heartedly," or "with all my heart." In spite of the dowry struggles, they did eventually marry, and their son became a prominent figure in the court of Henry VIII. Anyone interested in seeing the letter can view the manuscript online through the British Library's website.[20]

Whether those were the actual "firsts" or not, it does seem clear that a romantic Valentine's Day emerged in the late Middle Ages and that other traditions developed from there. The beginnings were English and aristocratic, with connections to the continent of Europe; eventually, Valentine's Day spread to other social classes and extended to the Americas and around the world.

It is difficult to identify exactly when and by whom various romantic embellishments to the legend of Saint Valentine were added. However, any mentions of Valentine performing underground weddings, or falling in love with the jailor's daughter, or writing a note signed "from your Valentine" emerge *after* the era of Chaucer, in some cases much later. Not to be too cynical, but it appears that once Valentine's name became associated with an annual recognition of romance, people were desperate to find some aspect of Valentine's life and legend that would explain the association. If nothing could be found in the historical record, human imaginations managed to make things up.

Admittedly, this revision of the conventional history of Valentine's Day certainly complicates my suggestion that the five holidays in this book are like three-layer cakes. It worked better when I thought Valentine's Day was rooted in a spring fertility observance dating back to the Roman empire or before (layer one) and then Christianity added its overlay with a focus on Saint Valentine (layer two). I admit that this may be a stretch, and I may be trying too hard to make my analogy work, but I think the layers still could apply to the revised history. With a beginning in the late Middle Ages, through Chaucer and friends, the holiday was essentially seasonal, a spring celebration of mating associated with nature and birds, and also applied to people. Even if it did not reach back to ancient civilizations and may not have had common origins across many cultures, the Chaucer origin of Valentine's Day was nevertheless as a spring observance (first layer). Then, because the Valentine name was superficially associated with the day of romance, a gradual attempt was made over several centuries to augment the life story of Valentine by adding romantic links (second layer). Such efforts may have been an attempt to enhance a Christian connection and give credit and attention to Christianity, but if the intention was to co-opt the holiday, it was never very successful. Christians could feel comfortable with the love theme of Valentine's Day because love is a religious theme as well, but Saint

Valentine's life and example were hardly the center of attention at any stage in the history of Valentine's Day. The second layer, if there is one, has always been tenuous. In contrast, the third layer, the commercialization that came with modern popular culture, has been overwhelming.

CARDS AND COMMERCIALIZATION

As Valentine's Day traditions grew and spread, and also rose and fell, they involved more than love letters and poems. Among the aristocracy, the day often provided an occasion for giving expensive gifts, including jewelry, and for enjoying extravagant banquets and parties. Among wider populations, the Valentine's Day rituals that developed over the next few centuries involved many folk games of matchmaking and playful attempts at divining future love interests. These ranged from choosing a partner for a parlor game by drawing names out of a bowl, to plucking flower petals to learn if someone's love was true ("he loves me, he loves me not . . . "), to placing an herb under a pillow in hopes that one's dreams would show the face of a future lover. Similar romantic folk customs became associated with many special days around the year, including May Day, New Year's Eve, and several saints' days. Valentine's Day was especially prominent among these days of matchmaking and divination, but another significant example, surprisingly, was Halloween, and examples of that will be considered more fully in the chapter on that holiday.

Whatever additional activities became associated with the day, a central feature of Valentine's Day continued to be the custom of exchanging written expressions of affection with loved ones. The form of these expressions has changed, from personally written poems and letters, to handmade decorative cards, to commercially manufactured cards with printed verses. Regardless of the form it took, the practice of sending expressions of affection was the catalyst that spread the popularity of Valentine's Day from England to the United States and from adults to families and children. Other features, like flowers and candy, dinner and gifts, followed.

Valentine's Day made a dramatic appearance in the United States in the 1840s. Prior to that, if Valentine's Day appeared at all in the American press, it was to note in passing a custom observed in Europe. While activities surrounding a great variety of saints were common in Europe, few saints' days transferred to the United States. One reason was that the vast majority of Christians in the United States prior to the mid-1800s were Protestants who tended to oppose many aspects of Catholicism, including the veneration of saints. Another reason was the tendency of the developing American ritual calendar to give more emphasis to days of civic remembrance, such as George Washington's birthday. Thus, American author Samuel Woodworth wrote in 1832 that the "English custom of sending *valentines*, and drawing lots for husbands and spouses, on the 14th of February, was never much practiced by the people of the United States, and is now almost unknown."[21]

In the 1840s that suddenly changed, mainly with a torrent of cards. The precedent had been set in England, where printers had begun producing valentine cards commercially around the turn of the century. Now that a person could purchase a card instead of writing a personal poem or note, card exchanges took off dramatically. Estimates claimed that 200,000 cards were being exchanged in London alone by the mid-1820s, a number that doubled over the next twenty years. By 1867 the estimate was one million.

The craze crossed the waters to the United States, with estimates in New York of 15,000 cards exchanged in 1843; 21,000 in 1844; and 30,000 by 1847. Similar dramatic growth was reported in cities like Boston and Philadelphia.[22] On February 14, 1849, Emily Dickinson wrote to her cousin about the flurry of cards and letters around her: "The last week has been a merry one in Amherst, & notes have flown around like, snowflakes."[23] Esther Howland of Massachusetts has been hailed as the Mother of the American Valentine because she produced some of the first elaborate American valentines in 1848 and eventually founded the New England Valentine Company, but as these numbers reveal, the fad already was well under way, what with

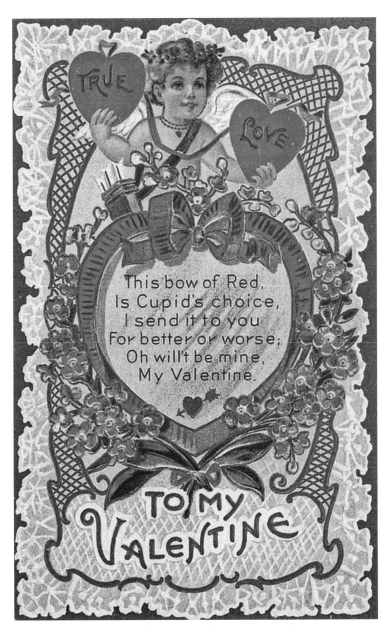

TRUE

LOVE

This bow of Red,
Is Cupid's choice,
I send it to you
For better or worse;
Oh will't be mine,
My Valentine.

TO MY
VALENTINE

Chromolithographed paper valentine created between 1880 and 1890.

imports from England, personal hand-written cards, and at least basic valentines produced by other Americans.

Three aspects of valentine exchanges in this era were quite different from today's ritual. One was that the individually written notes were indeed exchanges, so that if a man sent a poem to a woman expressing his interest and asking her to be his valentine, she would be expected to reply, either positively or negatively. This did not happen in just one day, so the valentine period informally extended over a week or so as one side composed and sent a note and then waited for a reply.

A second unique aspect was the assistance provided by pamphlets called "Valentine Writers." These were little booklets of varying length that were sold by printers and contained ready-made poetry for those who felt their composition skills were inadequate. The pamphlets appeared in England and later in the United States, in the time of transition when valentines were a mixture of personally composed notes and preprinted cards, allowing participants to send an individually written note while using someone else's words. Some pamphlets were specifically for men, some for women; some were for both. Many provided not only initial Valentine's Day poetry but also possible responses. One example from England was *Richardson's New London Fashionable Gentlemen's Writer, or, the Lover's Own Book for This Year Containing a Very Choice Selection of Original and Popular Valentines with Appropriate Answers*, published in Derby sometime in the 1830s. Richardson's also sold a companion booklet for women. Here is a sample, with two possible answers.

FROM A COTTAGER TO HIS FAVORITE LASS

I for my Valentine have got
A little comfortable cot;
I've got a little piece of land,
And other things too at command:
Oh, tell me then if you'll be mine,
Say if you'll be my Valentine.

ANSWER OF COMPLIANCE

To my thanks you have a claim,
For the kindness which you proffer:
I should be indeed to blame,
Were I to reject your offer.

ANSWER OF REJECTION

'Tis not land that can impart,
A good temper, a good heart,
In the cottage we may find,
Anger and a troubled mind.[24]

Another difference between Valentine's Day then and now is that in the past, a large number of valentines were sent anonymously. For many recipients who received endearing notes or cards, it was fun and exciting to try to guess who the secret admirer was. The experience might be compared with the practice of having a "secret Santa" at Christmastime, but with more romantic overtones. On the other hand, the anonymity also explains the existence of another kind of valentine common in the mid-1800s, those that were comic, satirical, or downright insulting. The texts and illustrations could be humorous, mocking, cutting, and/or sexually suggestive. Unlike most of the humorous greeting cards today, a number of these earlier cards were intended to rebuke or insult, ending with lines like "you will never be my valentine." In a period that saw the beginnings of struggles for women's rights, some valentine cards condemned women who ventured out of their expected roles. When I first saw samples of some of the especially mean-spirited cards I wondered who would send them. The answer is that they were sent anonymously. Satirical or caustic cards were numerous. In 1858 in the United States, *Harper's Weekly* estimated that Valentine's Day cards were evenly divided between sentimental and satiric, with about one and a half million cards in each category.[25]

The dramatic proliferation of valentines in the United States in the mid-1800s provided many opportunities for marketing and profit. Printers and stationers engaged in heavy newspaper advertising, created elaborate store window displays, and sponsored carnivals of activity within their stores. They successfully expanded the appeal of valentines from single adults and married couples to family and friends in general, including children. They provided cards for all kinds of relationships, both affectionate and adversarial. And over time, the loving expressions extended beyond cards to gifts.

For those who are disturbed by the commercialization of holidays, Valentine's Day could be considered the culprit, the wedge that prepared the way for what happened with Christmas and Halloween. As summarized by historian Leigh Eric Schmidt, "The valentine craze of the 1840s and 1850s proved the rehearsal for that great fashion of the late 1870s and early 1880s, Christmas cards. . . . The valentine trade thus helped inspire a whole new holiday enterprise, the greeting-card industry." By the 1920s, "Greeting cards had become the common accoutrement of almost any holiday or life passage."[26]

Although there is a common suspicion that Hallmark was behind it all, that well-known company actually arrived on the scene somewhat later. Founder Joyce C. Hall was born in 1891 in the small town of David City, Nebraska. (He was named for Methodist bishop Isaac Joyce, who happened to visit David City on the day of his birth, and he preferred to be called J.C. instead of the feminine-sounding Joyce.) After a boyhood selling picture postcards in rural Nebraska, he moved to Kansas City and with two of his brothers eventually established Hall Brothers, Inc., which became Hallmark. Interestingly, when he started selling greeting cards wholesale in 1913, he began with valentine cards, adding Christmas cards two years later, thereby replicating the chronological order in which the card crazes had developed in the 1800s. When World War I interfered with the importation of European greeting cards into the United States, Hallmark moved into a

Valentine's Day card, American, c. 1910.

position of dominance. "Christmas, birthday, and Valentine's Day cards were early best-sellers, but Hall wanted to manufacture cards that expressed virtually every sentiment for any occasion."[27] One of his many innovations was installing long card racks in stores, so that customers could browse instead of asking clerks to bring out particular cards from behind a counter. The entire enterprise, with cards, gifts, and television movies, was phenomenally successful, and by the time Hall died in 1982, Hallmark was valued at about $1.5 billion. Hallmark did not start the flurry of cards, but the company certainly built upon, encouraged, and profited from it.

With the addition of dinners, candy, flowers, and other gifts, Valentine's Day now ranks as the second highest grossing holiday in the United States, behind Christmas, approximately tied with Mother's Day, and ahead of Halloween and Easter. The National Retail Federation's annual survey predicted 2014 Valentine's Day spending to top $17 billion dollars, with males spending almost $170 on average and women spending about half as much. Matthew Shay, NRF president, commented that "Valentine's Day will continue to be a popular gift-giving event, even when consumers are frugal with their budgets. This is the one day of the year when millions find a way to show their loved ones they care."[28]

The breakdowns of spending are revealing. Eighty-nine percent spend money on their spouse or significant other, but people give cards or gifts to many others as well: children, parents, and other family members (59 percent); friends (21 percent); children's classmates and teachers (20 percent); pets (19 percent); and coworkers (12 percent). In terms of what people purchase, 51 percent send cards, 48 percent buy candy, 37 percent give flowers, 37 percent spend an evening out, 19 percent give jewelry, 15 percent give clothing, and 14 percent give gift cards. Fun facts regarding candy, one of the major purchases: more than 36 million heart-shaped boxed of chocolates are produced and sold each year, as are 8 *billion* of those little candy hearts with messages. As for valentine greeting cards, approximately 142 million are now exchanged each year, *not* counting the packaged boxes of cards for children.

One of the most stunning but not unexpected statistics reveals how extremely popular Valentine's Day is for engagements. In 2013, approximately 6 million couples in the United States became engaged on Valentine's Day. Considering that about 14 million engagements take place each year, that means that more than 40 percent of them took place on a single day. With an average price tag of approximately $2,500 for an engagement ring, those couples certainly help raise the spending averages for Valentine's Day.[29]

"Commercialization" has become the overriding word we use to summarize the cumulative impact of all these developments on Valentine's Day over the past two centuries. Not only has commercialization influenced the way Americans observe the day, but it has also served as a forerunner for similar developments with other special days, especially Christmas and Halloween.

HEART OF THE HOLIDAY

At the conclusion of a talk about Valentine's Day that I presented on a college campus several years ago, a science professor raised his hand and asked, "Where did the heart symbol come from?" Stalling for time, because I had no idea, I asked if there was any special interest behind his question. "I'm a biologist," he said. "I have held a heart in my hand, and it looks nothing like the valentine shape we call a heart." It was a question that had never occurred to me, and all I could say was "Good question."

Now I know more, but the answer is tangled and untidy. If you troll the internet, two theories appear to be most popular. One, the most risqué, is that the stylized heart is based on the shape of a woman's bottom, bent over. None other than Sheldon, on the television show *The Big Bang Theory*, is among the authorities endorsing this explanation. Similar suggestions have pointed to a variety of other portions of female and male anatomy. The problem with this approach is that the links with body parts are based on simple conjecture, without supporting historical evidence. Anyone can look at the shape of the modern heart logo and claim that it is similar to one section or another of the human body and then *guess* that the resemblance might explain the origin.

The other common theory is that today's stylized heart arose from the shape of ivy leaves or other plants that were part of the symbolism of ancient Greece and Rome. For example, one historical Greek coin pictures the head of Athena on one side; on the other is what appears to be a heart but is actually an ivy leaf. Other ancient coins from the city-state Cyrene, centuries before the time of Christ, portray the seedpod of a now-extinct plant, silphium, that was very important to Cyrene's economy and was sold as a spice and as a mode of birth control. The shape of the seedpod looks exactly like what we now call a heart shape. The symbolic meanings of these plants and leaves varied considerably, and the link with the later stylized heart is again speculative. In addition, we have no idea how or why the plant shapes would have turned red in the Middle Ages.

I have several friends in the field of medicine who claim that all of this speculation is based on a false premise, because they believe that the human heart does indeed look very similar to the stylized red image, and thus there is no need to resort to other theories. A number of academics agree. If you remove the distracting connections to the aorta and veins, the basic human organ of the heart has two sides (admittedly not quite symmetrical), rounded at the top and somewhat pointed at the bottom, with a pink color that can be viewed as bright red when considering the blood that flows through it. Art historian Martin Kemp raises an apt comparison by referring to the familiar logo of a smiley face. The well-known image certainly does not look exactly like a human face, but the two dots for eyes and the simple curved line for a smile are similar enough to a human face that we easily make the connection. That is how such iconic images work, providing a simplified, stylized representation of a more complicated reality. "A minimal level of resemblance is enough" for most icons, says Kemp, and that would seem to apply here as well.[30] Perhaps the simple answer is the best: the heart symbol is based on the anatomical human heart.

However, when did images of the modern red stylized heart arise? Surveying art history, the earliest appearances of what is essentially our modern iconic red heart emerge in the late Middle Ages, from two quite different sources. One is playing cards, with the heart as one of the four basic suits, along with clubs, diamonds, and spades. Documents from the 1370s refer to playing cards being introduced into Europe from the Middle East. Early handmade playing cards featured suits that varied by region, with very different designs, but the four suits that eventually became standardized for much of Europe and the United States were the French version. Their images certainly represent a courtly or chivalric era, with Kings, Queens, Jacks, and Jokers, and the hearts, clubs, diamonds, and spades became figures that also appeared on heraldry.

The second source was the Christian image of the Sacred Heart. The mental visualization of the crucified Christ, with blood flowing from his pierced heart, received great focus in medieval Christian spirituality. As summarized by art historian Martin Kemp, "Christ's 'Sacred Heart' became one of the most central images in Christian devotion, particularly in popular Catholic depictions of Christ in the printed media. It was complemented by devotion to the Virgin Mary's 'Immaculate Heart,' which followed in its train." Texts encouraging this devotional focus date back to the 1200s, and pictorial images of the heart began appearing at least by the 1400s. Many works of art picture a heart alone, nailed to a cross, or a bright red heart on the outside of the body of Jesus. Although the heart frequently was pierced by a lance or nails and was bleeding, by then its basic shape was in the form of the modern icon, and it was red. Over the following centuries, "the Sacred

Heart displayed in or on Christ's breast has become one of the most popular of all devotional images."[31]

These sources of heart imagery arose in the same general era as did Valentine's Day, and they coalesced in unclear ways to create a stock image, a pictogram that thereafter might be displayed for sacred or secular purposes or both. It became the central image for Valentine's Day, and it has been ubiquitous ever since, showing up in cartoons, advertisements, paintings, and on bumper stickers. Again in the words of art historian Martin Kemp, it is "a shape that is appealing in its simple yet seductive rhythm, and once seen it is difficult to forget. It is like the melody of a great pop song."[32]

Beyond the various ways the heart has been pictured visually, the history of its underlying symbolic meaning is long and complicated. Without diving too deep into the histories of philosophy and science, it is fair to say that many cultures, over many centuries, have in one way or another seen the heart as representing the inner being of a person, both physically and emotionally. In some cases in classical antiquity, the heart was considered the body's most important organ, but much of the discussion was anatomical rather than symbolic or metaphorical. One cultural historian claims that the understanding of the heart took an "emotional turn" in the high Middle Ages, when "the symbolic heart gradually separates off from the physical. Heart and love become one. . . . The heart is not the organ of love in a physical sense but a symbol and a synonym for love."[33] And what was the general context in which this emotional turn took place? It was the era of courtly love. Today we refer to the heart as a center of feelings and affections, most strongly as a symbol of love, and these associations date back to the very period when Valentine's Day began.

I believe it is appropriate to conclude a discussion of Valentine's Day with some attention to the heart, because it can help us understand why Valentine's Day has been embraced by so many people. This is not a complicated idea. If I am correct that the heart is the central symbol of Valentine's Day, it

Sacred Heart of Jesus, lithograph by Nathaniel Currier, c. 1845. The Sacred Heart was one of the forerunners of the valentine heart.

points to the themes of love and relationships. If Valentine's Day has become one of America's most culturally dominant holidays, it must be because we in the general public value love and relationships, and we are eager to affirm them.

One of the most basic principles in the analysis of popular culture is that popular culture both influences and reflects us. Popular culture surrounds us wherever we look—it's on television, in books, on billboards, in stores, online, and, well, everywhere—and it certainly influences or shapes us in ways that are sometimes obvious and sometimes subtle. However, that is not the whole story. It is also true that we, the general public, make choices that determine whether something becomes popular or not. Many new movies and television shows are not successful even when they are heavily advertised, because we do not respond to them. So when something becomes popular, we could say that it reflects us, because we made it popular, and our choices are an indication of what we like, or what we yearn for, or what we need. We are not mere pawns manipulated by corporations or mass media. We may be influenced by them, but our decisions and behavior influence them in return.

When faced with the commercialization of Valentine's Day, it is too easy to claim that this is something that merchants and advertisers have done to us. Indeed, we undoubtedly have been influenced by advertisements and peer pressure, and there certainly are other ways to observe Valentine's Day besides buying things. Yet there must be a reason that so many in the American population choose to participate in the day's rituals, when some other holidays are not nearly as successful commercially. Valentine's Day provides a special occasion for us to recommit to one another. The president of the National Retail Federation undoubtedly has an agenda behind his public pronouncements, but in this case he may be correct when he proclaims (as quoted above), "This is the one day of the year when millions find a way to show their loved ones they care."

Easter

Many Christians consider Easter the most spiritually important day in their annual ritual calendar, because it is a celebration of the resurrection of Jesus, which is central to the Christian message. However, have you ever stopped to think about the name of the day? Why is it called Easter? Why not Resurrection Day, or if two words are one too many, some other single word that points more directly to the day's event? Why "Easter"? What does the word mean, and where did it come from?

Historic Easter postcard, 1900.

The explanation is a winding road, with several detours leading to the eventual answer. It is an interesting journey that involves the Jewish observance of Passover and how it developed, early Christian controversies about how to commemorate the crucifixion and resurrection of Jesus, and changing symbolism and cultural practices as Christianity spread throughout Europe and into the Americas. The early part of the story is seriously religious but eventually involves bunnies, eggs, and Easter parades. As Shakespeare asked, "What's in a name?" The answer is, a lot.

PASSOVER

The first part of the answer, a surprise to many, is that a huge number of Christians do *not* call the day Easter. Growing up as a Protestant in the United States, I remember wondering why my Greek Orthodox friends called it Pascha. "Pascha" is the Greek version of the Hebrew word "Pesach," meaning protection, more commonly translated as "Passover." And lo and behold, except for English- and German-speaking people, almost all other European Christians refer to the resurrection day by using terms that derive from the Greek or Hebrew:

Spanish—*Pascua*

Italian—*Pasqua*

French—*Pâques*

Portuguese—*Páscoa*

Romanian—*Paşti* or *Paşte*

Danish and Norwegian—*Påske*

Swedish—*Påsk*

Dutch—*Pasen*

Icelandic—*Páska*

In essence, the special day that many of us call Easter, many other Christians call Passover. The first step in understanding Easter is to review how it is rooted in Passover, which itself was derived from preexisting spring rites.

To summarize briefly, Passover is the annual Jewish observance, celebrated in the spring, that remembers the exodus, the deliverance of the Hebrew people from slavery in ancient Egypt more than three thousand years ago. "Passover" refers to an event recounted in the biblical book of Exodus. As told there, Moses sent a message from God to the Egyptian pharaoh to let the Hebrew people go, and when the pharaoh refused, God unleashed many plagues upon the people of Egypt. The tenth plague was an angel of death sent to kill, in one night, the firstborn child of every family in Egypt and every firstborn animal. Moses instructed the Hebrew people to sacrifice a lamb and to smear the lamb's blood above the door of every Hebrew home, so that the angel of death might "pass over" that home and spare the child. Passover thus remembers the protection of firstborn Hebrew children and the larger story of the escape of the Hebrew people from Egypt, the well-known tale that also includes Moses parting the Red Sea.

Just as some Christian rites grew out of preceding seasonal observances, the same is true of the Jewish Passover. However, the exact details are murky; there are enough scholarly theories about the prehistoric roots of Passover to make anyone dizzy. This is understandable, since the further back one goes, the more limited the evidence, and thus it is necessary to speculatively reconstruct the story from fragmentary data. One academic who reviewed the wide range of theories about what preceded Passover concluded that "there is hardly any consensus among scholars. It seems that the only points of convergence are its annual character, spring as the season in which it was performed and its antiquity, although even for them there are opposing positions."[1] Three themes are highlighted in this statement: an annual observance, spring, and antiquity. This means there is at least a general scholarly consensus that the Hebrew people participated in some kind of annual spring ritual even before their departure from Egypt, but the central meaning of the spring ritual in those earlier years could not have been about the Passover story, because it had not happened yet.

We don't know exactly what the earlier spring observance was like. Spring was the season, so that may suggest some possible answers, but not the ones that immediately occur to many Americans. Keep in mind that spring in the Mediterranean region we now call Israel or Palestine means something quite different from the images that arise for most Europeans and North Americans. In my case, living in the American Midwest, spring means that I have survived another hard winter, and I celebrate the melting snow, the chance to wear a lighter jacket, the sounds of birds returning from their southern migrations, and the appearance of green grass, spring flowers, and budding trees as signs of new life. The early Hebrew people lived in a region that had no such dramatic change of seasons. Spring for them was in the first month of the Hebrew year, Nisan, which is around March or April in today's commonly accepted calendars. Because the region did not have a hard, cold winter, harvests of various crops occurred year-round, and spring would have celebrated the first of several harvests. The first harvest may have been of barley or similar crops. The point is that in the Mediterranean region, spring was not the emergence of life from the dead of winter, but it was the beginning of a new year.

In an example of one of the many theories surrounding Passover, Theodor Herzl Gaster has argued that when the particular meanings of the exodus story are removed, "The rites and ceremonies of Passover as described in the Bible find parallels in many parts of the world and fall into a pattern characteristic of primitive seasonal rituals." He especially emphasized the common meal, a ritual feast perhaps associated with a harvest where participants recommit themselves to one another and to the divine; such meals can be found in early cultures across the globe. The purpose of the meal "was to establish ties of kinship, revitalize the family or clan, and, by the assurance of divine protection, promote the increase of livestock and crops for the coming year."[2]

Whatever the details, some kind of a spring observance already existed as an established tradition before the time of the exodus. After the departure from Egypt, Judaism transformed the specific meanings of the spring ritual to focus on remembrance of the dramatic events of the liberation of the Hebrew people from slavery in Egypt. They did so believing that the observance was a direct commandment from God. The major narrative of the flight from Egypt is found in the biblical book of Exodus, especially chapters 1 to 15. As described there, when God gave instructions to Moses and Aaron about the slaughter of lambs and spreading blood on the doorposts, God said, "This month shall mark for you the beginning of months; it shall be the first month of the year for you." Also, "This day shall be a day of remembrance for you. You shall celebrate it as a festival to the Lord; throughout your generations you shall observe it as a perpetual ordinance" (Exodus 12:14). When the Israelites were brought out of the land of Egypt, Moses then repeated these instructions to the people: "Remember this day on which you came out of Egypt, out of the house of slavery, because the Lord brought you out from there by strength of hand; no leavened bread shall be eaten" (Exodus 13:3). The instruction echoes throughout additional passages in Hebrew scripture: "Remember that you were a slave in Egypt, and diligently observe these statutes" (Deuteronomy 16:12). Judaism therefore took a preexisting spring ritual tradition and, reinforcing it with such scriptural passages, gave it new meaning.

Closely associated with Passover was the Feast of Unleavened Bread. In some biblical accounts and external sources they are the same, but in others they are considered as two related festivals, mentioned side by side.[3] Whether one or two festivals, they seem to have arisen from earlier agricultural or nomadic rituals involving a meal, and they eventually provided two of the central Passover symbols, lamb and unleavened bread. After the exodus, lamb represented the sacrificed animal whose blood saved the Hebrew children. Unleavened bread, or matzoh, represented the haste with which the Hebrew people had to leave Egypt: they fled before their leavened bread had a chance to rise, leaving matzoh as the only bread available to them for their journey. The spring seasonal observance became a seven-day Passover celebration, and a meal featuring lamb, matzoh, and a recounting of the holy acts of God that freed the Hebrew people from slavery in Egypt became its centerpiece.

When a Holy Temple existed in Jerusalem, it was supposed to be the only place where sacrifices could be offered properly (Deuteronomy 12), and thus, if possible Jews were supposed to travel to Jerusalem for their Passover activities. However, after the Second Temple was destroyed by Romans in 70 CE, the Passover celebration gradually dispersed and became centered in the home. What resulted and exists to this day has been described as "the outstanding home festival in Jewish life."[4] It also is sometimes called the Feast of Freedom and the Spring Festival (Chag Ha-Aviv).

As currently practiced, Passover (Pesach) is a seven- or eight-day festival. A summary is somewhat complicated, because many details vary depending upon whether a person is Orthodox, Conservative, or Reform and living inside or outside Israel. The first day or two and the last day or two are full-fledged holidays in which people take time off from work and evenings feature festive meals in the home. Participants often return to jobs and other aspects of normal daily life in the middle or intermediate days. No leavened bread (chametz) is to be consumed during the seven or eight days, and one of the rituals of preparation in the days before Passover is to remove any chametz from the home. The more observant a Jewish family, the more thorough the housecleaning, which can involve scrubbing kitchens (including the insides of appliances) and replacing shelf liners, all to clean or remove anything that has even touched leavened bread in the past year. In many homes, on the evening before Passover a ritual search for unleavened bread becomes a family activity. Pieces of chametz are hidden throughout the home and family members search to remove them with a candle and a feather, or in modern days, a flashlight and a broom. Sometimes the chametz that has been collected is ritually burned the next morning.

וְאַחַר כָּךְ יְקַיֵּם הַמִּצְוָה הַשְּׁלִישִׁית הִתְחַתְּנוּת.יבצענה לשנים ויתן עליה לאתונא ויאכל ביחד בלא ברכה אֶלָא כָּךְ אָמַר בֵּן עֲשֵׂה חָלָל בִּזְמַן שֶׁבֵּית הַמִּקְדָּשׁ קַיָם חָיָה בּוֹרֵךְ מַצָה וּמָרוֹר בְּיַחַד וְיֹאכַל כְּמָה שֶׁ מַצּוֹת עַל מְרוֹרִים יֹאכְלֻהוּ

Passover Seder service. Woodcut from a medieval Haggadah.

Yet the centerpiece ritual of Passover, best known these days even to those outside the Jewish community, is the Seder, the family banquet held on the first night of Passover. More than just a sumptuous meal with lit candles and four cups of wine, it is a highly structured ceremony following instructions in a book called the Haggadah, collected and written sometime in the late 100s CE. The ritual involves fourteen or fifteen steps, including songs, poetry, prayers, ritual washing, and a recounting of the exodus story. Several steps involve eating specific foods and explaining their symbolic meaning, for example, salt water to remember the tears of Jewish slaves, and of course, matzoh. Many aspects of Passover have changed or evolved over time, but from seasonal beginnings to today there is a continuity in the common meal, with symbolic food, a remembrance of holy history, and a recommitment to God, family, and community.

CHRISTIAN PASSOVER

Then came Jesus of Nazareth and the emergence of Christianity, rooted in Judaism. If anyone needs to be reminded, Jesus was a Jew. He had Jewish parents. He read Jewish scripture, learned from Jewish teachers, spent almost all of his time with other Jews, shared most Jewish beliefs, and participated in Jewish practices, including Passover. Almost all of his initial followers were Jews. When a community of Christian believers emerged during and after the lifetime of Jesus, Roman leaders tended to see them as a sect within Judaism. When Christianity expanded further and became recognized as a separate religion, to a great extent it was a continuation of Jewish beliefs and practices, with some important new wrinkles. That is why, after all, when Christians eventually codified their book of sacred writing, they included the entire Jewish Bible (calling it the Old Testament) as well as some new additions (the New Testament).

In the four gospel narratives telling of the life and teachings of Jesus, Passover is the context at more than one crucial point. The only biblical story about Jesus as a boy tells of the family traveling to Jerusalem. When his parents lost track of him, they found Jesus "in the temple, sitting among the teachers, listening to them and asking them questions." Why had the family come to Jerusalem? "They went up as usual for the festival" of Passover (Luke 2:41–46). Later, when Jesus began his public ministry, one of the most dramatic incidents was when he drove money changers out of the temple, and Passover once again was the occasion. According to the scriptural narrative: "The Passover of the Jews was near, and Jesus went up to Jerusalem. In the temple he found people selling cattle, sheep, and doves, and the money changers seated at their tables." He overturned their tables, poured out their coins and told them to "stop making my Father's house a marketplace!" The Gospel of John concludes the narrative of that episode by noting, "When he was in Jerusalem during the Passover festival, many believed in his name because they saw the signs that he was doing" (John 2:13–23). It is clear that Passover was a central feature of Jewish life in that era, regularly drawing people, including Jesus, to Jerusalem.

However, the central connection with Passover was the series of events leading up to the crucifixion and resurrection of Jesus. All four of the gospels in the New Testament describe Passover observances in Jerusalem as the general setting, although they differ from each other on some significant details.

Scholars have called the three gospels named for Matthew, Mark, and Luke "synoptic gospels" (meaning "seen together") because they tell very similar stories and probably relied on crossover sources. These three gospels offer parallel descriptions of a last supper that Jesus shared with his disciples, followed by the events leading to his crucifixion, all in the context of Passover in Jerusalem. For example, from Luke:

> Then came the day of Unleavened Bread, on which the Passover lamb had to be sacrificed. So Jesus sent Peter and John, saying, "Go and prepare the Passover meal for us that we may eat it." They asked him, "Where do you want us to make preparations for it?" "Listen," he said to them, "when you have entered the city, a man carrying a jar of water will meet you; follow him into the house he enters and say to the owner of the house, 'The teacher asks you, "Where is the guest room, where I may eat the Passover with my disciples?"' He will show you a large room upstairs, already furnished. Make preparations for us there." So they went and found everything as he had told them; and they prepared the Passover meal. (Luke 22:7–13)

When Jesus and his disciples gathered at the table for the meal, Jesus said, "I have eagerly desired to eat this Passover with you before I suffer," and then took the wine and bread and offered words such as "This is my body which is given for you. Do this in remembrance of me" (Luke 22:14–20). Obviously, such words became the basis for the Christian ritual of Holy Communion. According to these three similar gospels, the Last Supper of Jesus with his disciples was a Passover meal.

The chronology here is that the lamb was sacrificed in the temple on the day of preparation, the day before Passover. However, unlike the common understanding today that days start and end at midnight, Jewish days were and are measured from sundown to sundown, and thus evening is the beginning of a new day. So the lamb that was sacrificed prior to sundown (the day of preparation) was then consumed on the first day of Passover (that same evening), and this was the last supper of Jesus with his disciples. That means that the events that followed—in other words the arrest, trial, and crucifixion of Jesus—would have happened within the seven days of Passover. Read Matthew 26–27, Mark 14–15, and Luke 22–23, and they all tell essentially the same story.

The Gospel of John is different. One thing that surprises many Christians, if they look closely, is that John's narrative includes no Last Supper, at least not as traditionally understood. That is because this gospel says that Jesus was crucified earlier, on the day of preparation, the day before Passover began (John 19:31). When Joseph of Arimathea, a follower of Jesus, made burial arrangements, the concluding sentence is, "And so, because it was the Jewish day of Preparation, and the tomb was nearby, they laid Jesus there" (John 19:42). Apparently it was important for the Gospel of John that Jesus be crucified at exactly the same time that the Passover lamb would be sacrificed, on the day of preparation prior to the first day of Passover, to make the point that Jesus was the new sacrificial lamb, offered up for the good of others. Thus, by John's chronology, Jesus could not have had a Passover meal with his disciples because Jesus was crucified before Passover technically began. The Gospel of John does mention a meal with disciples, but because of the timing it is not a Passover meal, and the meal does not include any of the familiar words such as "take and eat" or "do this in remembrance of me."

Details like this are what prompt arguments among Christians about how to interpret the Bible. Some see the Christian Bible as historically accurate in all its passages; others see some portions of the Bible as symbolic spiritual affirmations not intended as literal history; and additional views cover a wide spectrum in between and beyond. Settling such controversies is far beyond the scope of this book. The point here is that whatever the variations between the four gospel narratives, they all portray the crucifixion and resurrection of Jesus as occurring at least in the general time period of the Jewish Passover in Jerusalem. That is why the annual Christian observance happens in the same approximate time of the year as Passover.

In addition to timing, there is a second and even more important reason that many Christians refer to their annual observance as Pascha or Passover: the symbolism of the sacrificial lamb. If the blood of the sacrificed Passover lamb was what saved the Hebrew children, early Christians saw this as an ideal symbol to communicate the importance of Jesus. The Gospel of John states that John the Baptist called Jesus "the Lamb of God who takes away the sin of the world" (John 1:29). The first letter of Peter declared that "you were ransomed . . . with the precious blood of Christ, like that of a lamb without defect or blemish" (I Peter 1:18–19). For Christians, Jesus was the new sacrificial Passover lamb who saved humanity.

Christianity eventually developed an annual ritual calendar with many special days: Christmas, Ash Wednesday, Easter, Pentecost, All Saints' Day, and so on. Out of all of these annual special days, Easter, or Pascha, was the first to develop. However, it took a while, and it involved controversy. Some Christians believed that the annual observance should be tied exactly to the Jewish Passover, and thus the memorial of the death of Jesus should occur on the night from the fourteenth to the fifteenth day of the Jewish month of Nisan, the beginning of Passover. Those Christians were called

Quartodecimans (or Fourteeners), because of the date. Others thought that a celebration of the resurrection of Jesus should take place on the Sunday following Passover, because the gospels all seem to indicate that the resurrection of Jesus took place on the first day of the week, in other words, Sunday. Note that the disagreement is not just about the date; they disagreed about what should be emphasized most. All Christians gave attention to both the crucifixion and the resurrection, and the two are tied together, but which was most central to the Christian message? Crucifixion, Jesus dying for the sins of humanity? Or resurrection, the triumph of Jesus over death? (If you think about it, when you put them together, there is a bit of emotional whiplash involved in trying to emphasize crucifixion and resurrection at the same time.) Those who emphasized the crucifixion preferred the Passover date, and those who emphasized resurrection preferred Sunday. When Constantine became the first Roman emperor to embrace Christianity, he was disturbed that Christians were arguing so much among themselves, including over the date of Easter/Pascha. So he called together Christian leaders from throughout the empire to hash out their differences. The Council of Nicaea in 325 became the first of seven major Ecumenical Councils in early Christianity. Among many influential decisions made at Nicea, one mandated Sunday as the proper day for Easter.[5]

There are two questions people often ask about the dates of Easter, and both involve calendars. I admit that whenever I try to understand some of the variations among calendars, my head hurts. In this case the two questions raise two different calendar issues, which makes things even worse. The first question is, Why is Christmas on a specific date but Easter moves around? In the case of Christmas, Jesus and the religion of Christianity were born into the Roman empire, which had begun operating on the Julian calendar, a solar calendar with seven-day weeks and twelve months. A solar calendar is based on the earth's relation to the sun at different times of the year. Most of us still operate on a very similar calendar today. Christians eventually decided they wanted to celebrate the birth of Jesus on a specific month and day, December 25, based on the Julian solar calendar, and that date continues to be used today. No problem.

However, when it comes to Easter, the link with Passover causes some complication. The Jewish calendar existed before the Julian calendar, and it is a lunisolar calendar, one that is similar to a solar calendar in many ways but that also takes some account of the phases of the moon. (The Islamic calendar, by the way, is different even from that, because it is a totally lunar calendar.) For Christians, even after they decided to celebrate the resurrection of Jesus on Sunday every year, they still wanted their observance to be at least close to Passover. For Jews, Passover is celebrated on the first full moon following the vernal (or spring) equinox. That very description indicates the combination of a solar calendar and a lunar calendar. The reference to the vernal equinox is part of a solar calendar, and the reference to a full moon is part of a lunar calendar. Dates from a lunisolar calendar do not fit neatly into a solar calendar; when they are translated into a solar calendar, they vary from year to year. The Council of Nicaea added another factor: Sunday. For Christians, Easter is on *the first Sunday following* the first full moon following the spring equinox. Passover might begin on any day of the week, but Easter must always be on Sunday, so Passover and Easter may be closer to each other in some years than in others. This probably is more of an explanation than most of us need, but the result is that Easter may fall on dates anywhere from March 22 to April 25.

The other frequent question is this: Why do most Catholic and Protestant Christians celebrate Easter/Pascha on one date, but Eastern Orthodox Christians (such as Greek Orthodox, Russian Orthodox, and Syrian Orthodox) observe a different date? In this case, at least everyone is dealing with a solar calendar. The difference here is between the Julian calendar and the Gregorian calendar. Jesus was born under the Julian calendar, which had been introduced under Julius Caesar in 46 BC (or BCE). The calendar worked well for many years, and all Christians operated under it until the late 1500s. The Julian calendar had a tiny problem, however; measured by the movement of the sun, it was off about eleven minutes per year. As years went by, those minutes added up. After 134 years it was off by a whole day, and the discrepancy kept growing. In 1582 a new calendar was decreed by Pope Gregory XIII (thus the name Gregorian calendar) that made adjustments to fix the problem. The new calendar gained acceptance gradually; in some cases it took hundreds of years. One of the last countries to adopt it was Greece, in 1923. Today most countries, and most Catholic and Protestant churches, operate under the Gregorian calendar. Yet many Orthodox churches do not, even in countries where their governments do. For them, using the Julian calendar is part of an overall attempt to maintain the holy traditions of the church. Over time, some Orthodox churches have compromised on the date of Christmas, observing it at the same time as western Christians (Catholic and Protestant), using the Gregorian calendar. However, when it comes to Easter, almost all Eastern Orthodox churches hold to some version of the Julian calendar and celebrate Easter on a variable date later than the date celebrated by western Christians. The difference is not in the basic way they calculate Easter; that is almost the same, with slight technical variations. The main difference is that one group of Christians is using the Gregorian calendar and the other is using the Julian calendar to determine each year's date for Easter.

Now do you understand why my head hurts?

Before leaving this discussion of the Jewish and the Christian Passover, let me add one other aside about modern practices. I am aware of a number of Christian churches that in recent years have invited a rabbi or other Jewish representative to lead members of their congregation in a Seder meal, as a way to understand the Last Supper from a new perspective and to foster positive Jewish-Christian relations. I have participated in several and they were very meaningful experiences. However, we should note that the ritual meal called the Seder that is practiced in Jewish communities today is somewhat different from what might have happened in the time of Jesus and his disciples, in at least two ways already suggested here. In the time of Jesus, the Passover meal was centered in Jerusalem and did not necessarily revolve around the family. The wonderful family-focused celebration that we know today developed later, after the destruction of the Temple in Jerusalem. In addition, today's Seder ("seder" is a Hebrew word that means order) is in most instances a reading and acting out of the Haggadah, a Jewish text that most scholars agree could not have been written earlier than the late 100s CE, about 150 years after the lifetime of Jesus. Many of the elements included in the Haggadah might have been common practice long before then, but this *particular* ritual, its specific order and details, was regularized in this text, which has been influential ever since. For that reason, some people would call the Last Supper of Jesus and his disciples a Passover meal, but they would reserve the term "Seder" to refer only to meals taking place after the writing of the Haggadah. I fully understand that for many people these may be minor technicalities. Even if today's Seder is not exactly like the meal in the time of Jesus, it undoubtedly is similar. Participating in a Jewish Seder today can enhance a Christian's understanding of the heritage that surrounded Jesus, even if some modern details are different.

EASTER?

After all this consideration of Passover and early Christianity, the question with which we began still remains. Unlike so many others, why do English- and German-speaking people use the term "Easter" to refer to the annual celebration of Jesus's resurrection? For most of my life it never even occurred to me to ask what the word meant. Now, talking with people who apparently were more curious than I was and who had bothered to ask, the most frequent answer is that the word derives from the name of a pre-Christian spring fertility goddess. Is that true? The answer is maybe.

The claim about a goddess is based almost totally on writings by two men famous enough that their names are widely recognized. The first is Bede, often called the Venerable Bede, a British monk and eminent scholar who lived from about 673 to 735, in a transitional time when England had become at least nominally Christian but had a history and continuing remnants of previous religions. Bede entered a monastery at the age of seven and basically lived there his whole life. He was the author of over sixty books, and he had access to what was considered at the time a remarkably extensive monastic library, holding an estimated 200 books. Best known for his *Ecclesiastical History of the English People,* he was the first major historian to make use of the Anno Domini (AD) numbering of years. Thereafter it became increasingly common for Christians to designate years as BC or AD, with the life of Jesus as the center point for numbering the years. Bede did not invent this system of numbering, but he was the first major historian to use it, and his influence may deserve credit for launching it into what has become widespread use today.

The claim that the word "Easter" comes from a pre-Christian goddess named Eostre is based on two sentences that appear in Bede's book *The Reckoning of Time.* In a very short section, about two pages long, Bede listed the Old English names for months in the culture's previous lunar calendar, and he included the following statement: "Eosturmonath has a name which is now translated 'Pascal month,' and which was once called after a goddess of theirs named Eostre, in whose honour feasts were celebrated in that month. Now they designate that Pascal season by her name, calling the joys of the new rite by the time-honoured name of the old observance."[6]

That is it. Two sentences. In other words, Bede wrote that the month in which English Christians were celebrating the resurrection of Jesus had been called Eosturmonath in Old English, referring to a goddess named Eostre. And even though Christians had begun affirming the Christian meaning of the celebration, they continued to use the name of the goddess to designate the season.

These two sentences have given rise to controversy ever since Bede wrote them. Some skeptics doubt the claim, suggesting that Bede made it up. Undoubtedly some of the skepticism comes from Christians who do not want to see the celebration of the resurrection of Jesus tainted by any association with a pre-Christian religion or goddess. Yet their skepticism may have some justification, because virtually no corroborating evidence has been found, in narratives by other writers of the time or in archaeological objects, to support the existence of an annual feast for a goddess named Eostre—no art, no carvings, no religious objects. Bede's two sentences seem to be the only evidence, and later claims about the goddess almost always rely on Bede's testimony. On the other hand, those who argue in support of Bede's assertion ask why he would want to fabricate something like this. He was a Christian advocate who wanted to displace other religions. What would be his motivation for making up a non-Christian goddess?

If some Christians have been nervous or skeptical about Eostre, other observers have gone too far in the other direction and assumed that Bede said more than he did. The two sentences provide the name of a goddess and mention feasts for her. Bede provides no description of the goddess; he does not even say she was a fertility goddess, although that might be inferred from the spring season. Bede says nothing about any association with eggs, or hares as an animal totem, or any other details sometimes asserted by recent authors. Anything beyond Bede's two simple sentences are later speculative additions.

More than a thousand years later, another influential author reignited interest in this goddess: Jacob Grimm. The Brothers Grimm (Jacob, 1785-1863, and Wilhelm, 1786-1859), best known for their fairy tales, were extremely close, working together and living together for most of their lives. For much of the time they worked in the same room, at facing desks, and when Wilhelm married in 1825, his wife simply moved into the house where both brothers continued to live. Both were scholars, folklorists, interested in history and language, and both were nationalists who hoped that their folktales would enhance appreciation of a German heritage. They published eight books together; Jacob wrote twenty-one additional books on his own, and Wilhelm fourteen.[7]

In 1835 Jacob Grimm published *Deutsche Mythologie*, translated into English as *Teutonic Mythology*, in which he noted and defended Bede's assertion about a spring goddess. Using a process of "linguistic reconstruction," he went further and claimed that Eostre was basically the same as the Germanic goddess Ostara. The evidence Grimm used to support the idea was language, finding what he regarded as similar names for goddesses of the dawn in earlier Indo-European languages and cultures and concluding that they all *seem* to refer to the same goddess. Critics allege that this is all very speculative and that Grimm was embellishing Bede's claim to make up a German equivalent, Ostara. A key part of Grimm's case did indeed rely on Bede. Grimm argued that if even Christians continued to use the name in relation to their central festival, it must be an indication that there was a deeply rooted belief in such a goddess. In Grimm's words, "This Ostara, like Eostre, must in heathen religion have denoted a higher being, whose worship was so firmly rooted, that the Christian teachers tolerated the name, and applied it to one of their own grandest anniversaries."[8]

This idea of tracing linguistic roots is interesting, and even if it is not direct evidence of a goddess, it can point to some general themes. "Easter" has the same root as the word "east," the direction, and some linguists have traced it back thousands of years to meanings of "shine" or "dawn." It is not hard to put all of this together. The sun rises in the east. Sunrise is the beginning of a new day, new light, new life. Then apply this to a year instead of to a single day. The lengthening days, the increasing light, the dawn of a new year and the beginning of new life, all of these themes point to spring. Thus it may be enough to say that the word "Easter," like "east," linguistically carries the meaning of dawn, spring, and new life.

Or Easter may point to a specific spring goddess in Old England.

Or maybe both.

In any case, English- and German-speaking Christians have been comfortable appropriating this circle of words and symbols to point to the new life or resurrection of Jesus. Notice, however, that the geographical context shifted as the story moved from the Mediterranean setting of Israel or Palestine north to the England of Bede or the Germany of the Grimm brothers. Bede and the Grimms lived in the land of cold, hard winters where everything seemed to die, only to awaken in the spring. In that setting, spring meant something more dramatic in the north than just a new year. It meant life arising out of death, which could provide even more powerful symbols for the resurrection.

For Christians, Easter's central observance was worship, remembering and celebrating the resurrection of Jesus. It also expanded to become an entire season, with Lent as a forty-day season of preparation, beginning with Ash Wednesday, and a whole week of special days immediately preceding Easter, called Holy Week by western Christians and Great Week by Eastern Orthodox Christians. Palm Sunday and Good Friday stood out in that week, in remembrance of the triumphal entry of Jesus into Jerusalem on Palm Sunday and his suffering and death on the cross on Good Friday. Not just Easter itself but the whole cycle surrounding it was the first portion of what eventually became a Christian ritual calendar with special days and seasons throughout the year.

Throughout its evolution, other cultural elements surrounded or accompanied the worship experiences of Easter. From the earliest beginnings Easter was a spring event, and so, understandably, those additional cultural elements tended to be related to that season. This is very similar to the evolution of Christmas. When Christianity moved from the Mediterranean into central and northern Europe, the December 25 celebration of the birth of Jesus encountered all kinds of preexisting midwinter parties, and elements of

Resurrection of Christ, by Giovanni Antonio Bazzi (known as Sodoma), sixteenth century.

those often were incorporated into Christmas festivities. The same is true here. When Easter observances were introduced into new cultures, previously established spring symbols and practices frequently became associated with the religious holiday. That is how Easter became associated with images in addition to the cross, such as the Easter bunny, or colored eggs, or Easter parades. They are representations of spring, sometimes with ancient roots, amplified in modern popular culture, now fused with the Christian holiday.

RABBITS AND EGGS

So, what do rabbits and eggs have to do with Easter? The simple answer is that both are spring symbols representing fertility. Of course, there is more to say about each.

Consider the rabbit. The discussion here refers to both the Easter hare, usually found in Europe, and the Easter rabbit, more common in the United States. For most of my life, I have referred to rabbits and hares interchangeably, assuming they are the same. They are not. Let's digress briefly into a little zoology lesson, because it is interesting, but also because the American preference for rabbit is symbolically significant.

If you see pictures of a hare and a rabbit, they certainly look similar, and they are of the same order of mammals, *Lagomorpha*. However, they are completely different species, with differences both in appearance and in behavior. Hares tend to be larger than rabbits, with longer hind legs, longer ears, and black markings. Because of their powerful back legs, hares tend to run (or hop) faster, up to 45 miles per hour. Hares make nests above ground, in the grass. Rabbits burrow underground, creating secure dens or tunnels. (One exception is the cottontail rabbit, which makes above-ground nests similar to hares.) Baby hares are called leverets and are born with hair and with their eyes open; within an hour they can move on their own and require very little attention from their mothers. Baby rabbits are called kittens, and the adult males and females are called bucks and does. The word "bunny" is a synonym for rabbit, but most people use the term to refer to young or baby rabbits. The kittens, or bunnies, are born without hair and with their eyes closed, blind and dependent on their mothers. Thus, it is a good thing that rabbits have underground dens, because the blind, dependent bunnies need more protection than the independent leverets do. Because of their physical differences, hares are more prepared to run, while rabbits hide. Hares spend most of their lives by themselves, pairing up only to mate. Rabbits are more social and live in colonies. Rabbits can be domesticated as pets. Hares are almost always wild. In terms of overall impressions, hares may appear odd and wiry, perhaps even a bit frightening, while rabbits are seen as cuddly and cute. We will return to that contrast shortly.

For all the differences, both represent fertility, because they breed and mature rapidly. The statistics for rabbits are especially dramatic. Their gestation period is only one month long, and mothers bear four to eight litters per year, although hypothetically it could be twelve, because a mother can become pregnant again within hours of giving birth. There could be up to fourteen babies in a litter, although the average is about six. Babies become sexually mature in only six months, already able to reproduce. The resulting numbers can be astounding. To get a sense of the quantities, consider a comparison with cats. Some animal shelters encourage pet owners to spay or neuter their cats, because one mother and her offspring, repeatedly multiplied, could theoretically produce more than 40,000 cats in seven years. These are numbers that do not take into account mortality and other factors; they are theoretical numbers about the highest reproduction mathematically possible. Dr. Dana Krempels of the University of Miami applied the same kind of computation to rabbits, and she concluded that one mother and her offspring could produce almost 95 billion, yes *billion*, rabbits over the same seven-year period. As she says, the number of cats "pales in comparison to what a rabbit can produce!"[9] Do I need to say it? That is why hares and rabbits are symbols of fertility.

Hares and rabbits appear often in ancient art and mythology all over the globe. Because some markings and shadows on the moon resemble the shape of a hare or a rabbit, cultures as diverse as those in China, India, Mesoamerica, and Europe have stories about moon rabbits or hares. For complicated reasons, rabbits have sometimes been associated with luck, both good and bad (which explains the rabbit's foot on a key chain as a token of good luck). Yet their most common symbolism has been of fertility, sexuality, and sensuality. A prominent example from Greek antiquity is Aphrodite, the goddess of love and beauty, for whom the hare was a sacred animal. In modern America, think of the Playboy bunny and Playboy's use of a stylized rabbit's head and ears as a corporate symbol.

How the hare began to be included in Easter observances is unclear, but writings from as early as the 1600s describe a tradition of an Easter hare bringing eggs to children. On the Saturday night before Easter, German children would prepare nests in which the Easter hare might leave colored eggs; nests were assembled in a child's cap, or in grass or straw. Children were told that the Easter hare left eggs for good children but not for bad, somewhat like practices related to Saint Nicholas. When German immigrants settled in Pennsylvania they brought the tradition of the Easter hare with them, and they proudly claimed credit for it. In the words of folklorist Alfred Lewis Shoemaker, "The Easter rabbit is perhaps the greatest contribution the Pennsylvania Dutch have made to American life."[10] (Note that the Pennsylvania Dutch are not really Dutch but German. The confusion comes from the word "Deutsch," which means German in the German language. When filtered into the English language people began saying Dutch, which is in actuality an entirely different nationality.)

One additional reason that the Germans can take credit for the Easter rabbit in America is that there were not a lot of competing Easter traditions in colonial times. Many other Christian groups in the American colonies gave little attention to Easter and its accompanying cultural trappings;

Puritans, the same group that disapproved of Christmas, were the reason. As described earlier, Puritans in England and in American New England wanted to purge Christianity of what they saw as Roman Catholic additions that were not justified by scripture. They also believed that the celebrations had become too rowdy. Thus, they opposed "Festival Days, vulgarly called Holy Days," including Christmas, Easter, and Lent.[11] For Puritans, the weekly celebration of Sunday, the Lord's day, was enough. This disapproval of Easter and Christmas lingered for a century or more among English-speaking Christians who had been influenced by these Puritan views, including Congregationalists, Presbyterians, Quakers, and some Baptists and Methodists. The Germans, however, unfettered by Puritan disapproval, were free to bring their Easter traditions to the new land. By the mid-1800s Easter observances, including aspects imported by the Germans and others, began to be adopted even by the reluctant Christian denominations. In 1868, for instance, the *New-York Daily Tribune* reported that "the Easter Festival, once allowed to pass almost unnoticed by our Knickerbocker and Puritan ancestors, is yearly more and more observed and was celebrated with greater interest than has hitherto been manifested."[12]

What is especially interesting is that when the Easter hare tradition crossed the ocean to the Americas, the name gradually changed from "Osterhase" or "Oschter Haws" (Easter hare) to the Easter rabbit. For a while, Americans used the terms interchangeably; eventually, the word "hare" dropped out almost completely, with common references today in the United States alternating between Easter bunnies and Easter rabbits. Whether the shift occurred intentionally or not, the zoological differences described above make it appropriate symbolically if children are to be the focus of the tradition. Hares are more wild and powerful, while rabbits, especially bunnies, can be adorable and cuddly. If the goal was to shift from a primary emphasis on fertility and sexuality to something more suitable for children, the bunny is an ideal symbol.

Kindergarten students from Tilden School with Easter display of eggs, rabbit, and Easter lily, 1938.

In fact, many influences in the nineteenth and twentieth centuries unrelated to Easter have helped the rabbit take on "a relatively new identity as a suitable childhood companion and child-friendly animal." Consider these examples from classic children's stories, folktales, and cartoons:

Lewis Carroll, *Alice's Adventures in Wonderland* (1865)

Beatrix Potter, *The Tale of Peter Rabbit* (1901)

Margery Williams, *The Velveteen Rabbit* (1922)

Thornton W. Burgess, *The Adventures of Peter Cottontail* (1941)

Robert Lawson, *Rabbit Hill* (1944)

Richard Adams, *Watership Down* (1972)

Rabbit, companion in A. A. Milne, *Winnie-the-Pooh* (1926) and Disney adaptations

Joel Chandler Harris, Br'er Rabbit in the Uncle Remus stories

Thumper, Disney movie *Bambi*

Bugs Bunny cartoons

Trix cereal rabbit

As noted by Tanya Gulevich, these rabbits are "cozy, clever, or magical," and "the Easter Bunny shares in these qualities." It is likely that "these imagined character traits inspire children's continuing affection for these fictional rabbits and their mythological companion, the Easter Bunny."[13]

What about eggs? Like rabbits, they represent springtime and fertility, but the egg has additional possibilities that relate even more to religious meanings. Especially in the case of Easter, they are symbols of new life, which is what resurrection is all about.

Some academic and popular discussions do their best to trace the Easter egg to specific earlier traditions from which Christians might have borrowed, such as Egyptian or Persian precedents. It is more helpful, I think, to keep in mind that there are certain symbols that have self-evident possibilities for religious meaning. They are called "general symbols" because they have been used by many religions throughout the ages, around the world. One obvious example of a general symbol is water. Water easily can represent cleansing, the washing away of impurities, maybe even healing, and a chance to start over. Water also is essential for life; most plants and animals would die without it. So is it any wonder that religions almost everywhere have used water to express religious meanings? Examples include baptism in Christianity, sacred rivers like the Ganges in Hinduism, stories of a great flood in several religions, and ritual washings as preparation for all kinds of religious ceremonies. Another significant example of a general symbol is the circle. Because a circle has no beginning and no end, it can represent infinity or eternity. It can represent unity or the whole, in contrast to something that is divided into parts. It can also signify rotations, such as the circle of the seasons, or the circle of life. Again, is it any wonder that the circle appears repeatedly as a symbol in many religions?

I would argue that the egg is like water or a circle; it is yet another example of a general symbol. It is spherical, with a shape similar to the circle just mentioned, and it has a hard surface that to all outward appearances looks lifeless or inanimate, like a stone. Miracle of miracles, it cracks open and a living being emerges! What could be more amazing than that?

Therefore, creation or emergence narratives from around the world often include an egg. Ancient Egyptian stories tell how the entire universe hatched out of an egg, and the egg plays a similar role in Hindu myths from India. In fact, the image of the world, or life, emerging from an egg seems almost universal, appearing in tales from Greece, Indonesia, China, Africa, Central and South America, and other places. In addition to representing creation itself, the egg also naturally signifies new life in the spring, fertility, and sometimes magical powers.[14] By the way, a hard-boiled egg is included in the Jewish Seder meal considered earlier, and although the egg's meaning has been interpreted in a variety of ways, the interpretations almost always include a theme of the beginning of life, for individuals and for the Jewish people. The widespread appearance of the egg is summarized by folklorist Venetia Newell: "All over the world, wherever eggs are laid, they represent life and fertility and are symbolic of creation and resurrection."[15]

In that context, the question is not how eggs came to be associated with Easter. Rather the question is, how could the obvious symbolism of an egg *not* become associated with the resurrection of Jesus, sooner or later?

It is difficult to identify when eggs first became identified with Easter, but evidence of Easter egg practices dates back at least to the Middle Ages.

One example is a record in 1290 from the reign of King Edward I of England for the purchase of 450 eggs in the Easter season, to be colored or covered with gold leaf and distributed to members of his royal household. There is evidence of similar activity in Poland, Austria, and tsarist Russia in the Middle Ages.[16] Decorated eggs became part of Easter observances as Christianity spread throughout Europe, into the Americas, and beyond, with variations from culture to culture.

In some parts of eastern Europe, especially among Eastern Orthodox Christians, Easter eggs are red. To explain the origin of the red egg, one common Eastern Orthodox tale (which has many variations) centers on Mary Magdalene, identified by the Gospel of Luke as one of the women who discovered the empty tomb after the resurrection of Jesus. It is said that she later obtained an audience with the Roman emperor Tiberius, to protest that Pontius Pilate had executed an innocent man. While it was the custom for people approaching the emperor to bring a valuable gift, Mary Magdalene brought a simple white egg and proclaimed, "Christ is risen!" As the story goes, the emperor replied that "rising from the dead is as impossible as a white egg turning red," and when he spoke those words, the egg turned red in Mary's hand. Some icons in the Eastern Orthodox tradition show Mary Magdalene holding a red egg. An alternate story says that the Virgin Mary, mother of Jesus, brought a basket of eggs to the soldiers guarding Jesus and asked that they treat him well. While she was pleading for her son, her tears fell on the eggs and they turned red. In these stories, red eggs represent Christ's blood and sacrifice or, when cracked open, the empty tomb. At the conclusion of some Orthodox Easter services, red hard-boiled eggs are distributed to all, and congregants move to a meal breaking their Easter fast. Each participant knocks his or her egg against the egg of another as a sort of game, seeing which egg cracks first, breaking them open as a part of breaking their fast. Whether in homes or in churches, baskets holding eggs all dyed a deep, bright red present a striking sight.

Also notable are the eggs beautifully decorated by folk artists from the Ukraine and Poland. Most of us have seen examples of these eggs, with their very exquisite patterns, and we wonder how such fine, delicate decorations are possible. The term for these eggs is "pysanky" (Ukranian) or "pisanki" (Polish), meaning "to write." Pysanky artists trace fine lines or designs of hot wax onto an egg and then lower the egg into a dye bath. The wax protects portions of the egg while the rest of the egg absorbs the color. This process can be repeated over and over again for multicolored patterns, and afterward the design is protected by a coat of varnish. The eggs are not hard-boiled, and when everything is dry, perhaps a day later, the artist pierces a tiny hole in each end of the egg and blows out the white and the yoke, leaving an empty shell. The designs on these eggs vary widely, from explicit Christian symbols to geometric patterns to birds, flowers, or any image the artist might choose.

However, it is the legendary Fabergé eggs that represent the height of elaborate egg decoration. This series of eggs was produced in tsarist Russia between 1885 and 1916. At that time, given the prominence of the Russian Orthodox Church in Russian culture, Easter was a major celebration of the year, both religiously and culturally, just as the Christmas holiday seems to dominate in the United States today. It had been a long-standing tradition for Christians to bring hand-colored eggs to the Easter worship service, where the eggs were blessed, subsequently to become gifts for family and friends. Russian royalty had built on this tradition, exchanging jeweled eggs, but Czar Alexander III wanted to do even more. He commissioned the court jeweler, Peter Carl Fabergé, to craft an exceptionally elaborate egg as a surprise for his wife, Czarina Maria Feodorovna, apparently for the Easter of their twentieth anniversary in 1885. Called the Hen Egg, it seemed outwardly to be a white enamel egg, but when opened a yolk of gold appeared inside. Within the yolk was a gold hen, and the hen in turn opened to reveal a miniature diamond replica of the imperial crown and a tiny ruby pendant. The empress was so delighted that Alexander commissioned a new

Woman painting Ukrainian Easter eggs, 1968.

egg annually, a tradition continued by his son Nicholas II (who ordered two eggs annually, one for his wife and one for his mother) until the Russian Revolution in 1917. Each egg took a year or more to make, even with a team of craftsmen working on each. While the designs were diverse, each egg had to have a surprise inside, such as a miniature jeweled coronation carriage, or a swan, or an elephant.

Fifty imperial Easter eggs were made, and forty-three survive. In March 2014, news broke about a scrap metal dealer from the American Midwest who bought an egg-shaped object at a flea market for $14,000, speculating that the value of the gold would be worth that much. It was not, but he then realized that the egg might be an important work of art. It has now been confirmed as the previously lost Third Imperial Easter Egg, featuring a small watch on a tripod pedestal, surrounded by gold, sapphires, and diamonds. Recently sold to a private collector, its value is estimated at $33 million.[17]

In the American experience today, the practice of parents and children dying hard-boiled eggs is a far cry from those elegant examples, but it is a fond childhood memory for many. The colors usually are pastels, for unknown reasons. One guess is that they reflect the colors of spring flowers. In addition to dying hard-boiled eggs and later eating them, the major related domestic activity in the United States is the Easter egg hunt, which takes place in the family living room or backyard, or on a church lawn, or is organized by a civic group in a public space.

Another Easter game is egg rolling, where eggs are placed at a starting line on the top of a hill and pushed, in a race to see which egg reaches the bottom first. On flat terrain, children might push the egg with a spoon. Some attempts to give this event a Christian meaning have suggested that the rolling egg represents the rock rolled away from the empty tomb of the resurrected Jesus, but for most people it is simply a children's game. The most widely publicized egg roll is the annual event held first on the United States Capitol grounds and later on the White House lawn. Begun as an informal activity before the Civil War, it has become an annual entertainment for thousands of children. (From the early years it was understood that no adult could attend the White House Egg Roll unless accompanied by a child.)

As we trace the cultural trappings of holidays in the United States and their expressions in modern popular culture, a common theme especially for Christmas, Halloween, and Easter is that they have become domesticated, made family friendly and, especially, safe and appealing for children. Historian Gary Cross claims that "after the Civil War, Americans reinvented Easter as a day commemorating youth and family" as part of a broader pattern of "infantilizing" many holidays.[18] Thus, our modern consideration of the Easter rabbit ends up mostly celebrating a lovable, magical Easter bunny appropriate for children. And the Easter egg tradition consists largely of family traditions of dying eggs and staging egg hunts for children, with the addition of Easter baskets and plastic eggs with candy, toys, or money inside, again for children.

This relates to a second theme, commercialization. In the words of Steve Olenski, a marketing blogger for *Forbes* magazine, "Let's face it. Easter is not exactly the proverbial hotbed of marketing and advertising when it comes to generating revenue. Despite all the confections and eggs and marshmallow-infused goodies, it's not even the best holiday for candy, with that honor falling to Halloween, of course."[19] Yet it is still a holiday with spending in the billions.

Surveys conducted by the National Retail Federation in 2014 indicated that US citizens would spend almost $16 billion on Easter, in the following categories: $5 billion for groceries or a meal out, $2.6 billion for attire, $2.4 billion for gifts, $2.2 billion for candy, and $1.1 billion each for flowers and decorations. Eighty-seven percent of American parents say that they prepare Easter baskets for their children. Eighty-one percent of Americans share or give candy for Easter. Jelly beans are especially popular at Easter, with 16 billion jelly beans produced for the holiday, but still, almost three-fourths of Easter candy is chocolate.[20]

Despite all of the attention given to Easter baskets, eggs, and candy, these statistics reveal that the two largest segments of Easter-related spending are food and clothing. The greatest expenditure, food, highlights the special importance of family meals, a topic discussed further in the Thanksgiving chapter. The gathering of family and friends for an Easter meal can be a centerpiece of the holiday, even for those who do not emphasize its religious importance. The ubiquitous Easter meal is a reminder that the cultural and commercial activity of the season involves persons with numerous, even contrasting motivations.

One Christian-based polling organization asked Americans about their personal view of Easter, and a majority saw it as a religious occasion. Replying to a free-response question, 67 percent gave answers such as "a Christian holiday, a celebration of God or Jesus, a celebration of Passover, a holy day, or a special time for church or worship attendance." Two percent volunteered that it was the most important holiday of their faith. That still leaves 33 percent who did not see Easter as religious, including 8 percent who did not celebrate Easter at all or who said it meant nothing to them. Nonreligious responses included viewing Easter as a time for getting family and friends together, a time for dying and hiding eggs, a time for children, and more, descriptions that those with religious responses might share as well.[21] Like Christmas, Easter is a religious holiday for some and a cultural holiday for others, and for many it is both.

The other consumer statistic, money spent on clothing, points to an area where the commercialization of the American Easter actually has receded. There was a time when the widespread American cultural expectation was for everyone to appear in a new Easter outfit when they arrived at church or the family dinner. Some Christian interpreters suggest that the tradition of new clothes arose from baptisms on Easter Sunday in the early church, where the newly baptized donned new white robes. Whether the tradition goes that far back or not, it is reasonable that persons who had survived winter would need new clothing for the spring, and making or obtaining that clothing could become associated with a spring festival like Easter. Various pieces of evidence suggest that Europeans associated Easter with new clothes prior to settlement in the American colonies. For example, an often-quoted old Irish aphorism stated, "For Christmas, food and drink; for Easter, new clothes." And Shakespeare, in *Romeo and Juliet*, has one character criticize another for wearing his new doublet before Easter.

In the United States the tradition's most prominent example became the Easter parade, which arose somewhat spontaneously in the 1870s and 1880s when parishioners from prominent New York City churches strolled Fifth Avenue following Easter morning worship services to show off their elegant fashions, especially ladies' hats, their "Easter bonnets." Irving Berlin enshrined the practice in his famous song "Easter Parade" (1933), which was followed by a movie with the same name, starring Fred Astaire and Judy Garland (1948). At its height in the late 1940s, the New York City Easter parade drew crowds estimated at over a million people, inspiring other parades in cities like Atlantic City, Boston, Philadelphia, and New Orleans. The parades still occur annually, although they are substantially diminished and are now more of a carnival featuring outlandish hats, instead of the fashion show of earlier years.

By the 1890s, the expectation of new clothes for Easter was being encouraged by explicit marketing appeals from merchants via newspaper and magazine advertisements, store windows, and other promotions. In 1894 one trade journal commented that "Easter is pre-eminently the festival of the dry goods trade. . . . Much of the success of the year's business hangs upon the demand experienced during the weeks just preceding Easter."[22] The expectations continued until recent decades, and many adults today, nationwide, remember the special Easter clothes of childhood. However, as Peter Steinfels of the *New York Times* has written, echoing the impression of almost everyone, "The whole association between Easter and clothes isn't what it

Easter parade: crowds in front of St. Patrick's Cathedral on Fifth Avenue in New York City on Easter Sunday, 1904.

used to be."[23] He suggests that the new spring fashions remain but are not as focused on Easter. Even more important, I would suggest, is that in today's American culture clothing is increasingly casual at work and at worship, influencing even Easter Sunday. If new Easter clothes drove sales in previous generations, that spending is greatly diminished now. When is the last time you saw an Easter bonnet?

So, Easter is a holiday with three layers, or four, depending on how you count. The first layer is a spring seasonal observance, and if Bede and Grimm are right about an early fertility goddess, the very name Easter is a reminder of that layer. The second layer, a religious overlay, has two parts. Judaism transformed an earlier spring ritual into Passover, remembering the exodus

Clothing in Easter window display, Dayton's, Minneapolis, 1957.

from Egypt, and Christianity built upon that, seeing the death and resurrection of Jesus as a new kind of Passover.

The third layer, modern popular culture, raised ancient spring symbols like rabbits and eggs to enhanced prominence, added an emphasis on family and children, and found itself susceptible to the same kind of commercial marketing that has accompanied other holidays. However, when compared to Halloween, Christmas, and even Valentine's Day, one could argue that the commercialization of Easter has been more restrained, and has perhaps even receded, in light of the declining emphasis on Easter clothing. Perhaps the significant Jewish and Christian religious messages of this season have inhibited a full commercial onslaught, recognizing that for a major segment of the American population, an Easter recommitment to faith and family remains paramount.

Halloween

One September a couple of years ago, a friend sent me a note: "Now that Labor Day is over, Happy Hallowthanksmas to you!" Indeed it seems like that. As soon as summer fades, the marketing starts for Halloween, and it continues as an unending blur through Thanksgiving and Christmas, with each

Dance of death with plague victims. Woodcut from the *Nuremberg Chronicle*, 1493.

holiday tumbling over the other. The first in line is Halloween, a holiday that did not exist in early America but has burst into importance in recent decades and is now one of the fastest growing holidays for consumer spending. Where did Halloween come from, and what has prompted its recent dramatic growth?

SAMHAIN AND ALL SAINTS

It is generally accepted that the American Halloween has Celtic roots, which leads most of us to think of Ireland. The culture is broader than that, with an early presence in much of Europe and now centering in what are often termed the six Celtic nations (not officially distinct nations): Ireland, Scotland, Wales, Cornwall, Brittany, and the Isle of Man. The point is that Celtic history and culture do not end at the borders of modern-day Ireland but extend to a number of neighboring geographical areas. Their Druid priests of pre-Christian times have been described in widely disparate ways, from lurid, frightening portrayals by early Roman and British historians to enthusiastic appreciation by modern-day neo-pagans. In the words of one commentator, they are seen alternately as "bloodthirsty pagans or paleo-tree-huggers."[1] A balanced depiction is somewhere in between, but little is certain, because their religious rituals were secret and whatever evidence is available now comes from archaeological artifacts or oral traditions. When oral tales were written down, the scribes were usually Roman conquerors or Christian missionaries, with their own perspectives filtering the information.

With those limitations, and understandable debates among historians, the likely predecessor of Halloween was a fall Celtic observance called Samhain (pronounced SAH-wen, although dialects vary). In some ways it was a new year's observance. That may sound strange, because in today's calendar, shared by most western cultures from Roman origins, a new year starts on January 1, but not all cultures see it that way. If you consider the seasons of the year, the choice of January 1 as the beginning of a new year seems somewhat arbitrary—it is a date in the middle of winter when there is no discernible change in weather or other natural conditions. Some early cultures instead divided the year into two halves, a light half and a dark half. Summer, with its warmth and crops, was the center of the light half, and winter was the center of the dark half. Viewed that way, the logical turning points in the year would be approximately May 1 and November 1. May 1, or May Day, marking the beginning of the light half of the year, has been a traditional spring fertility celebration in many lands and was embraced by Roman, Gaelic, Germanic, Scandinavian, and other cultures. November 1 then would be the end of the light half, a transition into darkness, cold, and hibernation. For the Celts, May 1 was called Beltane and November 1 was called Samhain, and they were the two most important days of the year. As crucial seasonal transitions, conceivably either one could be considered the beginning of a new year, but for the Celts it was Samhain. Not only was it a harvest celebration that followed the gathering of crops, it was also the time when livestock were slaughtered to thin the herds and prepare meat for winter. Celts would gather at the Hill of Tara, the seat of power of prehistoric kings, for three days of feasting, sports, legal trials, and settlement of debts, a year-end final accounting. Everything would be wrapped up and started over, marking the beginning of a new year.

This three-day celebration beginning on the evening of October 31 has been the subject of considerable debate and misinformation. One issue is the name of the celebration. Linguists have long agreed that Samhain means "summer's end." However, in 1786 a British military surveyor fascinated with the Celts, Charles Vallancey, wrote that Samhain actually was the name of a Celtic god, also called Balsab, meaning "Lord of the Dead." This claim has been repeated frequently, both in Vallancey's era and in recent years by some American Christians who oppose Halloween. The problem is that even in his own time, most scholars dismissed much of what Vallancey wrote as fabrication unsupported by evidence. Yes, the theme of death appeared in this fall observance, but references to either Samhain or Balsab as the name of a deity who is a Lord of Death appear nowhere else in ancient Celtic lore.[2]

A second debate is about whether Druids engaged in human sacrifice. At least three Roman authors, including Julius Caesar, writing about his Gallic Wars in Europe, claimed that the Druids offered human sacrifices to appease the gods. One of the most dramatic images is Caesar's description of a huge human-shaped wicker cage that held people who were burned alive: "Others use figures of immense size, whose limbs, woven out of twigs, they fill with living men and set on fire, and the men perish in a sheet of flame."[3] Skeptics discount the narratives as exaggerations by Roman conquerors trying to prove their civilized superiority over the tribes they defeated, and they suggest that the men may have been burned because they were criminals. Historian Nicholas Rogers takes a cautious middle position because of ambiguous, inconclusive information. In his words, "The idea that the Druids engaged in human sacrifice is not implausible, although the references to their activities are frustratingly fleeting."[4] However, even if the Druids did engage in human sacrifice, which is possible, there is no clear indication that it was a ritual especially associated with Samhain. It is certainly probable that livestock were slaughtered in the fall, perhaps as part of religious rituals but also in preparation for winter.

In spite of the historical uncertainty about what happened at Samhain, there seems to be agreement that it was a harvest festival, a time of legal settlements, and a very rowdy three-day celebration with feasting, drinking, games, and bonfires. And there was one other very important feature. The Celts believed that this was the one time of the year when the veil between earthly reality and the spirit world was especially thin. Ghosts of the dead might return to the natural world, and fairies (*sidh*) could cross over to pester humans. Such beliefs fit the season well; it makes sense that the end of summer and the approach of winter would be a distressing time, and howling winds and dropping temperatures did not help. With their attention focused on the spirits of the dead and on ghosts and fairies, the Celts countered dread and uncertainty with bonfires to push back the darkness, and perhaps with ritual dancing and masks or costumes, either to hide from the spirit creatures or to scare them away. This belief in a temporary opening between this world and the otherworld helps set the tone for what eventually becomes known as Halloween. Although we do not know with certainty the exact practices of those days, and thus we cannot trace them directly to specific modern Halloween customs, Samhain provides the background of annual harvest festivities that took place around November 1, approaching winter, in what was believed to be the brief time each year when ghosts or spirits inhabit the human realm, a special time combining boisterous celebration and darker themes of fear and death.

Then came Rome. Shortly before and after the lifetime of Jesus, Roman power had exerted itself and established some presence in what is now the British Isles. Christianity became the favored religion in the Roman empire beginning in the 300s, and within a century Christian missionaries such as (but not only) the legendary Patrick extended the religion into Ireland. That set the stage for Samhain to encounter a Christian observance, All Saints' Day, that would give Halloween its name.

The history of All Saints' Day goes back to the early centuries of Christianity, when Christians sometimes were persecuted in the Roman empire and put to death because they refused to worship Roman gods and goddesses. Those who died were considered martyrs, heroes in the faith, and served as an inspiration to Christians around them. Christians gathered the martyrs' bones as relics and created an annual ritual calendar to remember the day each martyr died. After Constantine became the first Roman emperor to accept Christianity and the persecutions stopped, the tradition of honoring martyrs continued, eventually widening to include other saints, persons designated by the church as exemplars of the faith. In the early Christian centuries, days dedicated to martyrs or saints tended to be local, devoted to remembering and praying to those well known in a particular region.

In 609 or 610 the Byzantine emperor Phocas, residing in Constantinople, gave Pope Boniface IV a building in Rome that most of us have seen in pictures, the Pantheon, and Boniface converted it into a church. The Pantheon had been filled with statues of Roman gods and goddesses, and on May 13 Boniface dedicated it instead to the Blessed Virgin (Mary) and all the martyrs. This can be considered the beginning of a Christian annual day dedicated to all the martyrs or saints. (The May 13 date applied only to the western portion of Christianity. The eastern church already had a ritual calendar with different dates for many observances.) The date is interesting, because in earlier centuries under the Roman empire May 13 had been the concluding date of the Lemuralia, a Roman feast during which restless and troublesome spirits of the dead were given offerings and exorcised. In essence, Romans were trying to expel ghosts or evil spirits from their homes. Did Boniface choose May 13 as the date of dedication to further emphasize that Christianity had fully replaced the former Roman religion, with an alternate recognition of those who had died? Maybe. There is at least a coincidence of dates.

More than a century later Pope Gregory III dedicated a chapel in St. Peter's Basilica to all the martyrs, and he changed the date of the anniversary feast from May 13 to November 1. That was for Rome alone, but in 837 Pope Gregory IV declared November 1 the official All Saints' Day for the entire western church. Why was the date moved from May to November 1? Numerous authors have assumed that it must have been to compete with or supplant the Celtic Samhain. Here is a place where speculation is tempting but some facts raise questions. First of all, as just noted, when Gregory III first changed the date it applied only to Rome, so he probably did not have the faraway Celtic people in mind. After Gregory IV applied it to the whole western church, Catholics in England did observe the November 1 date, but in Ireland the All Saints' commemoration initially was observed on April 20 and only later shifted to November 1. There are a number of other possible reasons for Roman Catholics to have moved All Saints' Day from May 13 to November 1. Maybe fall was a better time for Rome, because the fruits of a fall harvest would be available to feed the crowds that would pour into Rome to attend services. Maybe the end of summer and the beginning of winter, a seasonal change from life to death, is simply a natural time to think of the dead; similar practices appeared in many cultures, and perhaps Christians in western Europe were doing the same thing. It is too easy to assume that when Christian leaders established something on a certain date it was *always* a conscious attempt to compete with preceding non-Christian practices. In some cases that was true and in some cases not. Sometimes the motivations were mixed, and in many instances we just do not know. In this case, the claim that Christians moved All Saints' Day to November 1 only or mainly to compete with Samhain is questionable.

Whatever the motivation, November 1 became All Saints' Day, eventually in Ireland too, and a century later All Souls' Day was added on November 2 and became widely adopted in the western church by the 1300s. All Souls' Day was mostly a time of prayer on behalf of the dead who were in purgatory, temporarily between heaven and hell. If All Saints' Day was for the very holy people, All Souls' Day was for the rest of us. The result was a three-day period of special Christian observance. There was the evening before All Saints' Day, called All Hallows' Evening or Eve, and then the day itself, All Saints' Day, also called All Hallows or Hallowmas. ("Hallow" meant holy, and Hallowmas referred to the special mass on All Saints' Day, a name similar to Christmas.) All Souls' Day was on the third day, and the days together were called Hallowtide. By the late Middle Ages these were among the most important days of the Christian year. All Saints' Day became one of the Catholic six days of obligation, when the faithful are expected to attend mass, an expectation that continues today.

So this is how Halloween got its name, as a shortened form of All Hallows' Evening. The pre-Christian seasonal festivities at harvest time became concentrated in the evening before All Saints' Day, and the encounter with Christianity contributed the label for the celebration. The evening of October 31 became known as All Hallows' Evening or, when abbreviated, Hallowe'en.

When reformers broke from Roman Catholics in the 1500s, Protestants rejected almost all of these special observances for saints. (By the way, October 31 was the day that Martin Luther sent his famous *Ninety-Five Theses* to his superior; it is commonly believed that he also nailed the list to the door of a church where he lived. Was the choice of that day intentional?) Protestants believed that Christians had direct access to God (their doctrine being referred to as the "priesthood of all believers") and did not need to pray to saints or other mediators. They also disagreed with the idea of purgatory, seeing it as an unscriptural Catholic innovation. However, in Ireland and Scotland Halloween activities remained largely untouched, even among Protestants. Protestant efforts there were focused on other issues and apparently their leaders were content to leave popular cultural practices alone. Bonfires and torchlight parades continued to be held on the evening of October 31 in a combination of revelry and defensive activities to ward off evil spirits and witches. Belief in spirits and fairies blended with Christian beliefs and practices. Young men would roam the streets, drinking, singing, and soliciting gifts, and many young women would stay home and play parlor games trying to predict the future, especially regarding romance and marriage prospects. Halloween had become a standard part of Celtic folklore, an aspect of Irish and Scottish ethnic identity, and those who eventually emigrated to the New World carried it with them.

BLACK DEATH AND WITCH HUNTS

Before turning to the American Halloween, it is important to note two important occurrences in Europe in the late Middle Ages and following centuries that contributed themes and images to Halloween mythology. The first was the plague, later called the Black Death, which swept through Europe with terrifying results. In October 1347 a ship docked in the port of Messina, Sicily, to reveal most of its crew lying dead, their skin covered with black boils oozing blood and pus. Although some had heard rumors of this calamity in other parts of the world, no one understood what was happening medically or how it spread, and movement by trading ships and overland travelers brought infection to most of Europe within two years. In that century alone, from a total European population of about 80 million, an estimated 50 million died, more than 60 percent of the continent's inhabitants.[5] The disease was spread by rat bites, fleas, and the human cough. A person might look healthy one day and die the next, although the passage from infection to death usually took from six to ten days. The plague had ravaged England by 1349, and outbreaks continued off and on for three more centuries, with 20 percent of England's population dying in just one of its last epidemics, in 1665–1666. The plague terrorized Europe, isolating friends and relatives from one another as they attempted to avoid contamination. Disposal of bodies was difficult, with thousands dying each day, and the stench was dreadful. Those who believed that the plague was some kind of divine punishment sought to rid their communities of those who might be evil, leading to massacres of Jews and others considered foreign or unworthy. It also gave rise to a morbid sense of humor and a gruesome fascination with skeletons and paintings of the Dance of Death or the Dance Macabre, which became absorbed into Halloween imagery. As summarized by Halloween historian Lisa Morton, "The new common obsession with depictions of skeletal Grim Reapers found a natural home in a festival once thought to be the night when the dead crossed over into the world of the living."[6]

The second event in the late Middle Ages that contributed to Halloween traditions has been called a witch craze: the witch hunts that took place in the 1500s and 1600s in Europe and New England. Christian theologians had long struggled with the problem of evil, seeking to understand how bad things could possibly happen if God was both good and all powerful. Over the centuries heretics, sorcerers, and the Devil all received part of the blame, and witches came to be associated with all three. Trials of witches took place throughout the Middle Ages and were often used to accuse political or religious opponents, but the number of trials accelerated in the 1400s in the midst of social turmoil caused by the plague, the Hundred Years' War, and other factors. Accused witches became scapegoats. The *Malleus Maleficarum*, the most famous of several books that virtually became manuals for witch hunters, appeared in 1487. It was not an easy read—the thick volume had three parts and was written in dense scholarly language. As summarized by historian John Demos, "The first part lays some theoretical groundwork—by establishing that disbelief in witches is rank heresy, by showing the irrevocable connection between witches and the Devil, by canvassing the numerous harms (*maleficia*) they bring, and by tracing their usual biographical profile (with special emphasis on the female gender)." The second part of the *Malleus Maleficarum* described forms of witchcraft and principles of investigation, and the third part outlined legal steps to be taken against suspected witches.[7] Over the next two centuries this book and others like it had immense influence as hysteria about witchcraft proliferated.

Witch trials peaked between 1580 and 1650, in a period following the Protestant Reformation, but both Protestants and Catholics were actively involved in opposing witches and both employed similar approaches. Their use of torture brought many false accusations and confessions. Claims that as many as nine million witches were executed have been scaled back substantially in recent scholarship, to estimates of between 100,000 and 200,000 witch trials, with executions of approximately half that number of people, a number that is still disturbingly large.[8] Think of it: somewhere between 50,000 and 100,000 people died because they were accused of being witches. Many many others were affected by the witch hunts, including

Illustration depicting the burning of a witch at the stake in seventeenth-century Europe. Wood engraving, late nineteenth century.

persons who lived under suspicion but were never charged, the tortured, the accusers, the witnesses and judges, and all who were caught up in fear. In retrospect, it was not a period in European history of which to be proud.

Today's caricature or stereotypical image of a witch as an old hag riding a broom emerged in that era, but that does not describe all who were accused. Men as well as women, of all ages, were tried and executed, with great variations by region. Yet stereotypes often are built on partial truths, and an estimated 80 percent of the accused were indeed women, and a disproportionate number were older. The role of gender can be controversial, but it is hard to deny that European society at that time was male dominated, and that many males consciously or unconsciously were concerned about the hidden power and influence of midwives, female healers, and other women in nontraditional roles, and even of the sway of mothers within the family.

Consider the images associated with the stereotypical witch: a broom, a boiling cauldron (a kitchen kettle), and a black cat (a pet). All are domestic symbols of the kitchen, of hearth and home, but have been demonized.

Elaborations of Satan or the Devil developed considerably throughout the Middle Ages, with many names, such as Lucifer, Beelzebub, and the Prince of Darkness, and with images picturing him as part man and part animal, grotesque, and eventually sprouting horns and a tail. The witch trials tied witches directly to Satan, frequently accusing female witches of forming pacts with the Devil, of sponsoring gatherings with him on All Hallows' Eve, and of having sex with him. The *Malleus Maleficarum* includes a whole section of details about witches who copulate with the Devil or demons (incubi).[9] Women as the "weaker sex" were believed to be more vulnerable to demonic temptations, as demonstrated by Eve in the Garden of Eden, when she was enticed by the serpent to commit the first sin by eating the forbidden fruit. The common but false assumption today that witchcraft and Satanism are the same thing arises in part from the era of witch trials. It was not so much the pre-Christian roots of Halloween that brought about this alleged association between witches and the Devil; it was witch hunt hysteria centuries ago that did so, which many Christians now regret.

Scotland, one of the Celtic nations, had a proportionally large share of trials, with an estimated three to four thousand accused witches executed from 1560 to 1717.[10] The first major examples were the North Berwick witch trials, begun in 1590, which garnered a lot of attention because King James VI of Scotland presided over them himself. When dangerous storms interfered with Anne of Denmark's sailing to join him for their wedding, James became convinced that a coven of witches had conspired to prevent his marriage by supernatural means. Seventy people were accused in the plot, and torture produced both confessions and allegations against others. James later wrote a book about sorcery and witchcraft titled *Daemonologie*. In a union of crowns, this James VI of Scotland became James I of England in

1603, and only a few years later Shakespeare wrote his renowned play *Macbeth*, which includes Scottish kings, murderous plots, and witches. The trials of North Berwick incited ongoing fear of witches, prompting over two thousand additional trials in Scotland in the following years. Witches, the Devil, brooms, and black cats had become a part of Scottish culture.

Ireland, by the way, had very few witch trials, especially when compared with Scotland. Of course the American colonies were home to the famous Salem witch trials, but they arose near the end of the witch hysteria in Europe and quickly ended. Begun in the spring of 1692, the Salem trials resulted in the execution of nineteen people out of about 150 accused, but public support for them quickly waned, and a year later the trials were over. In 1697, public officials in Massachusetts, seeing the trials as a tragedy, declared a day of fasting. Justice Samuel Sewall publicly apologized for his role in the trials, and the Massachusetts legislature attempted to restore the reputations of the accused and provide financial compensation for heirs of the executed.

CELTS IN AMERICA

It was Irish and Scottish immigrants in particular who brought Halloween to America, and in the early years they tended to celebrate it as their own ethnic festival. As their practices were shared with neighbors of other backgrounds, and as the fall celebration merged with other autumn customs, it became an American national pastime.

American newspapers and almanacs in the late 1700s and early 1800s included virtually no references to Halloween, a festivity largely unknown in the young nation. Then came Irish and Scottish settlers, and their numbers were substantial. There had been a few Irish and Scottish citizens in colonial America and in the earliest years of the United States, but massive waves of immigration began in the 1840s and continued through the rest of the century. The Great Famine, also known as the Irish Potato Famine

(1845–1852), brought starvation and disease to Ireland when a blight decimated the potato crops upon which a third of the population depended. One million people died and another million left, many for the United States. In the following decades, until the United States passed restrictive immigration laws in the 1920s, wave after wave of Irish immigrants continued to arrive on American shores. The Scottish came too, although more of them settled in Canada. As summarized by historian Nicholas Rogers, "Thus, at the turn of the century, the Irish were the predominant immigrant minority in the United States; in Canada, the Irish and Scots outnumbered those of English extraction by a ratio of seven to five."[11] Historian Kerby Miller offers another dramatic comparison: "By 1900, more Irishmen and –women (including second-generation Irish-Americans) were living in the United States alone than in Ireland itself."[12]

Halloween in the Old World—in Ireland, Scotland, Wales, and England—had involved the activities mentioned above: bonfires; torchlight parades; young men wandering the streets, sometimes in costume; and young women at home, playing games of divination. In the United States, immigrants might have parties on the evening of October 31, imitating what they remembered of their former customs and telling nostalgic tales. Three Celtic contributions became especially significant parts of the American Halloween.

One was the jack-o'-lantern. In Ireland, small lanterns were created by hollowing out a turnip or a beet and placing a candle inside, to light the way as people ventured through the night. The flickering light from the lanterns looked similar to the flashes of light that arose from peat bogs or marshes, flashes that appeared mysteriously and vanished quickly and were believed to be ghosts or fairies. They are now explained as the result of the spontaneous combustion of gases from decaying matter, but back then they were given names like foolish fire, will-o'-the-wisp, or jack-o'-lantern.

Irish folklore included stories about Stingy Jack, a thief who tricked or trapped the Devil in various ways and then bargained to let Satan go if he would agree not to take Jack's soul. When Jack died, his sinful life made him ineligible for heaven, but the bargain he had struck with the Devil meant he could not enter hell. Satan did not like Jack much anyway, so when Jack complained that he had no way to find his way through the night, the Devil gave him an everlasting ember from the fires of hell. Jack placed it in his turnip lantern to guide his way, consigned to a fate of endlessly wandering the earth. He was Jack of the lantern. When the Irish came to the New World they found a new kind of squash, the pumpkin, native to North America and much larger than the turnip of old. The Irish quickly adopted the pumpkin as a replacement, again carving it and placing a light inside, creating what has become the bright orange symbol for the modern Halloween.

A second Celtic contribution was trick-or-treating, although it was not called that until later. There are many possible predecessors to the custom of going from house to house, but two traditions that had been adopted by the Celts in the old country were "souling" and "guising." Souling surfaced in relationship to All Souls' Day or the evening before, when the poor would visit homes asking for money or food; in return they would offer prayers for the dead, either to help release the dead from purgatory or simply to honor them. Among the foods they received were soul cakes, small breads or cakes they might eat fresh from the oven as they said their prayers. The cakes also could be set out to feed the ghosts of the departed in case they returned to earth briefly during these few days. A Celtic practice but one that could also be found in other parts of Europe, souling could be viewed as a way to help the poor, or to assist the souls of the departed, or to appease ghosts who might cause mischief. The custom is reflected in a common folk song from long ago, recorded in recent decades by musicians such as Peter, Paul and Mary and Sting; it is now often transferred to a Christmas setting:

A soul, a soul, a soul cake,
Hey, good missus, a soul cake,

An apple, a pear, a plum or a cherry,
Any good thing to make us merry,
One for Peter, two for Paul,
Three for Him who made us all.

Go down into your cellar and see what you can find
If your barrel is not empty we'll hope you will prove kind
We'll hope you will prove kind with your apples and strong beer
We'll come no more a-souling until this time next year.

Guising, or appearing in disguise, was simply the practice of dressing in costume, which may have had precedents in Samhain rituals of masquerading as demons or evil spirits. (Again, our information about earlier practices is limited.) As it developed in Scotland in particular, young adults in costume went door to door on the evening of October 31 to entertain by singing songs, telling stories, or performing sleight-of-hand tricks in return for something sweet. The two traditions of souling and guising only a day or two apart (one on October 31 and one on November 2) merged to become a Halloween tradition.

New Celtic immigrants in America reminisced about these practices, keeping them alive as a nostalgic ethnic memory, but they did not take to the streets in great numbers until near the end of the 1800s, when Halloween became a more national amusement linked with other harvest festivals and fall parties. Immigrants of other nationalities had similar traditions, such as the British Mischief Night on the eve of Guy Fawkes Day, or the German "belsnickling," visiting house to house in the Christmas season. Early America had problems with crowds of unruly young men roaming through towns on various festival days when they did not have to be at work; at least in this case it could be justified as part of a Halloween tradition. The crowds solicited food and money, but in many cases they were more interested in pranks, and the phrase "trick or treat" arose in that context. The first known published use of the phrase appeared in Canada in 1927, and the first appearance in the United States was in a 1934 Oregon newspaper that reported, "Other young goblins and ghosts, employing modern shakedown methods, successfully worked the 'trick or treat' system in all parts of the city." A 1937 item in an Indiana newspaper stated, "Trick or treat. This seems to be the popular pastime among the younger folk and Valparaiso people . . . will hear it many times tonight, for it is Hallowe'en."[13]

So-called tricks, seen as good fun by the perpetrators, were indeed carried out, but many recipients viewed this activity as threatening. Unhinging front gates and discarding them blocks away, overturning outhouses, or splashing paint on buildings were no laughing matter for many citizens. For instance, in 1905 the chief of police in Bristol, Connecticut, announced that he would increase police patrols on Halloween night to protect residents from "the persons, mostly boys, who have made life miserable for some years past." It was reported that he had "no objections to boys and girls celebrating the night in a reasonable manner, but when droves of youngsters march through the streets pelting citizens and houses with vegetables he will make somebody answer for it."[14] In sum, both the phrase and the practice of trick-or-treating emerged in the United States in the first half of the 1900s. A backlash prompted efforts to domesticate these practices, to make them safer and more family friendly, as described below.

In addition to the jack-o'-lantern and trick-or-treating, a third Celtic contribution to the American Halloween was divination. In the 1800s and 1900s, gender was important in how Halloween was celebrated, because men and women engaged in quite different activities. If young men gave Halloween a questionable reputation with their pranks, young women were occupied with other activities at home, activities now largely forgotten because the practices have disappeared. Their focus was divination, consulting the spirits or engaging in fortune-telling, mostly to learn what romances or marriages the future would bring. These home entertainments took place during other holidays as well, but they were especially associated with Halloween or harvest time in Ireland and throughout the British Isles, and they were common in the United States until the last half of the twentieth century. Many of these forms of predicting future romance were summarized in the poem "Halloween," written by the famous Scottish poet Robert Burns (1759–1796) to keep alive the old Scottish country customs of October 31. Sections of Burns's long poem were repeated at home parties throughout the next century, in Celtic lands and in America. In describing the matchmaking games, Burns at points had to stretch to find a variety of phrases to refer to romantic couples or future marriage partners; one somewhat humorous phrase was "your future conjugal yoke-fellow."

Several popular methods of divination involved apples. A girl would try to pare the skin of an apple in one long piece and then throw the peel over her left shoulder. When it landed, whatever letter was suggested by its shape was considered the initial of the name of a future love interest. Or a young woman could stick wet apple seeds on her cheek or forehead, having named each seed for a potential boyfriend. The first seeds to fall predicted unworthy suitors, while the seed that stayed on the longest was a sign of love or marriage. Another tradition was to gaze into a mirror exactly at midnight, holding a lighted candle, and in some traditions eating an apple, and a shadowy image of the woman's future husband would appear over her shoulder in the mirror.

Hazelnuts or chestnuts also were used to predict the future. Nuts named for possible lovers were placed in a fire, to learn which one burned the longest. Or two nuts representing a couple would be arranged touching each other in the embers. If they burned in place it was a sign of a long future together. If the nuts popped and jumped away from each other, the future was not promising. In Burns's poetic description, intentionally written in Scottish dialect, this was when "monie lads an' lassies' fates are there that night decided."

Some kindle, couthie, side by side,
　An' burn thegither trimly
Some start awa, wi' saucy pride,
　An' jump out owre the chimlie[15]

Yet another kind of ritual was described by Halloween historian Lesley Pratt Bannatyne. Some young women "believed that if they swallowed a thimbleful of salt before going to bed and didn't say a word, the one they would marry would give them a drink in the night. If he came with a gold cup, he would be very rich; with a silver cup, just well-to-do; with a wooden cup, very poor."[16] The examples could go on and on.

Yet as Halloween became a truly national festivity, it absorbed far more than just a Celtic inheritance. In the words of David Skal, "In reality, contemporary Halloween is a patchwork holiday, a kind of cultural Frankenstein stitched together quite recently from a number of traditions, all fused beneath the cauldron-light of the American melting pot."[17] A melting pot may not be the best image, however, if that implies that everything melded together into one homogenous mixture. A stew pot is more apt, where the meat, potatoes, and other vegetables are still identifiable, although mixed together and influencing one another.

Some of the things that Halloween absorbed were simply harvest traditions and the plants that came with them. From ancient cultures down to today, it has been an understandable human impulse to gather for celebrations after much of the work of the fall harvest had been completed, and it was no different for Native Americans and for the earliest European settlers in America. After the Celts imported their Halloween traditions, the celebration absorbed aspects of American harvest parties and plants native to the Americas. One example, the pumpkin, has been mentioned already. Another plant native to the Americas was corn, or maize. Indigenous peoples in Mesoamerica (the region now called Mexico and Central America) domesticated the crop long before Spanish colonizers arrived, and traders later exported it back to Europe and elsewhere in the world. Corn became the most widely grown crop in North America, eventually leading to harvest entertainments such as corn-shucking contests on the American frontier. Today dried corn stalks, husks, and ears of naturally colored corn are featured as decorations for both Halloween and Thanksgiving. And candy corn is one of the favorite Halloween treats.

Another Halloween staple is the scarecrow. Farmers around the world have resorted to all kinds of techniques to scare away birds and animals that might feed on their crops, and a constructed figure with a human appearance is one option. Scarecrows are associated with an entire growing season, not just the harvest, but what creates a potential link to Halloween is that they are supposed to be *scary*, or maybe even magical and otherworldly. That connection has been developed in popular culture and in American literature, for instance in Nathaniel Hawthorne's short story "Feathertop," published in 1852. It tells of a witch in Salem, Massachusetts, who brings a scarecrow to life for a romantic relationship that does not work out. The story was eventually adapted for several television shows and plays. *The Wonderful Wizard of Oz* and comic book superhero story lines feature scarecrows. Yet scarecrows do not seem to have become a Halloween standard until they began to be used in pranks in the early 1900s, when boys used them to scare girls. Scarecrows created grotesque human silhouettes in the dark, even headless figures, perhaps with replacement pumpkin heads.

Speaking of headless figures, the most famous is the headless horseman who frightens Ichabod Crane in Washington Irving's short story "The Legend of Sleepy Hollow," first published in 1820. That was before the arrival of masses of Celtic immigrants in America, and the word "Halloween" never appears in the story. However, it takes place in the autumn, it includes a harvest party, and the story itself is an example of one of the staples of fall gatherings around a fire: telling scary stories, and talk of ghosts. It even includes a shattered pumpkin in the last few pages. All of these elements

John Quidor, *The Headless Horseman Pursuing Ichabod Crane*, 1858.

were ideal for absorption into Halloween mythology as it developed in the 1800s and 1900s.

Some other Halloween symbols were apparently American contributions too, not European imports, although we do not know exactly how they developed. Black cats were associated with witches in Europe, but bats and owls seem to have been added in America, probably because both are nocturnal. Early Halloween parties were decorated in fall colors such as yellows and browns, but over time orange and black emerged as the unofficial standard colors in the United States. Can we guess why? Orange for the pumpkin, and black for night, darkness, and even death? By 1921 a Halloween guidebook effectively summarized the expected visual images for the American Halloween: "Decorations for Hallowe'en may vary greatly, but black cats, bats, Jack'o'Lanterns, ghosts and witches predominate. Autumn leaves, corn stalks, fruits and vegetables carry the idea of a harvest celebration. Orange and black crepe paper are indispensable in decorating."[18]

In the late 1800s and early 1900s, Halloween become a national celebration. As summarized by historian Nicholas Rogers, "In the mid-nineteenth century, Halloween had been regarded as a preeminently Irish or Scottish festival, as one observed by immigrants or first-generation Americans of Irish or Scottish descent. This notion persisted until the 1890s, when journalists still pondered whether the holiday would become anything more than an ethnic-identified festival. Yet as early as 1875, one newspaper noted that many Americans besides 'our Irish adopted citizens' were celebrating Halloween."[19]

Students at colleges and universities sponsored Halloween-themed parties. Social elites organized elegant Halloween balls, dinners, and country club gatherings, often attended in costume. Working- and middle-class families invited friends and neighbors into their homes for party games, including bobbing for apples, various parlor games, and divination for young adult women. Participants often viewed Halloween events as the continuation of an ethnic tradition, even if it was not of their own ethnicity. For Americans not of Celtic background, Irish and Scottish traditions were exotic. In 1919, librarian Ruth Edna Kelley wrote in *The Book of Halloween*, "The taste in Hallowe'en festivities now is to study old traditions, and hold a Scotch party, using Burns' poem *Hallowe'en* as a guide, or to go a-souling as the English used. In short, no custom that was once honored at Hallowe'en is out of fashion now."[20] The new national Halloween appealed to nostalgia for an older, simpler time. However, the evening also saw expanding activities by young men trick-or-treating through the town, which increasingly became a problem.

The subsequent development of Halloween involved many variations by region and local circumstance and even by decade, too many to list. However, I suggest that overall, the American Halloween has developed through three major phases:

1. Growth from a Celtic observance into an American national holiday, with rowdy public pranks as a growing problem
2. After 1920, domestication of the holiday to make it safe and family friendly, especially for children
3. In recent decades, the reentry of teenagers and adults into the festivities

We have examined the first phase; the second phase was a reaction against Halloween excesses.

HALLOWEEN FOR CHILDREN

Anoka, Minnesota, provides a case study of a community's attempt to do something about Halloween mischief. In a national context in which pranks seemed to be getting meaner and stories circulated about angry adults

Halloween

shooting buckshot at young people and chasing them in cars, Anoka's citizens were upset about some of the incidents that happened in their own community on the Halloween evening of 1919. An outhouse had been tipped over with someone in it, windows were soaped, and a horseless carriage was placed on the roof of Anoka High School. Most distressing of all, someone let loose a herd of cows that were found wandering Main Street the next morning, with one even making its way into the county jail. Another cow had been locked into a school classroom and "was reported to have eaten three history and two algebra books. Clearly, the citizens of the town had had enough."[21] Civic leaders formed a committee to address the problem and enlisted support from the local Commercial Club and Kiwanis chapter. To provide alternative activities for Halloween in 1920, they organized a city parade that included bands, the police and fire departments, civic clubs, and hundreds of children marching in costume, followed by a bonfire and the distribution of free popcorn, candy, and other treats. It worked, and the vandalism diminished. The next year they did it again and the parade drew thousands. Anoka has continued its annual Halloween parade and many auxiliary activities every year since then except for 1942 and 1943, during World War II. Today a suburb of Minneapolis with almost 20,000 residents, Anoka bills itself as the Halloween Capital of the World and draws about 70,000 visitors annually to its parades, concerts, fireworks, dances, races, and other activities. The city's website advertises that it was "the first city in the United States to put on a Halloween celebration to divert its youngsters from Halloween pranks." If it wasn't the first, it was certainly among the earliest. In the following decades, other towns and cities launched similar efforts to keep young people out of mischief on Halloween night by entertaining them with dances, parades, games, window-painting and costume contests, and parties, all sponsored by schools, churches, and civic organizations.

Another development that helped tame Halloween was the emergence of trick-or-treating as an activity for younger children. The focus was on collecting candy from house to house, with not a whiff of threatened tricks. We might assume that this children's activity was always a central part of Halloween, but that is not so. This new kind of innocent trick-or-treating began around the time of World War II and blossomed fully in the 1950s and 1960s. Until then, young children had been largely absent from American Halloween activities; almost all previous Halloween customs involved young adults and older ones. What began in the late 1940s with children wearing homemade costumes and collecting apples and popcorn balls from neighbors transformed quickly in the 1950s and thereafter to children wearing manufactured costumes representing the latest favorite television and movie characters and collecting candy. It was only then that candy manufacturers found in Halloween a target market and candy became closely associated with the holiday. Sales opportunities for costumes and decorations also increased dramatically. In the words of folklorist Tad Tuleja, Halloween became "simultaneously commercialized and infantilized."[22] Trick-or-treating by costumed children became the signature Halloween activity after World War II, a ritual especially well suited to growing suburban communities but also adopted in other settings. Informal community expectations developed about what age was too old to participate. With children going house to house, much of the pranking by young men was pushed aside, the home fortune-telling customs were discarded, and, as summarized by Halloween historian Lisa Morton, "The young people who had once enjoyed practicing those games were now confined to either the occasional costume party or handing out treats with older family members."[23]

However, it should be noted that, if the emergence of children trick-or-treating is an example of the domestication of Halloween, it is different from the domestication that happened with Christmas, Easter, and even Thanksgiving, because it was not centered on the home. Christmas, Easter, and Thanksgiving all feature the dynamic of coming home, of traveling to reunite with family and friends, with the gathering at a family meal as the centerpiece. In

Children trick-or-treating on Halloween, 1948.

contrast, Halloween sends children *out* from the home. It is a time for children's amusement and adventure out in the world, albeit often with careful supervision. Children's trick-or-treating, encouraged as an innocent alternative to earlier Halloween problems, may indeed have helped tame Halloween, but the holiday did not become one focused on home and family.

Yet another step toward a wholesome Halloween was the program to trick-or-treat for UNICEF, which many baby boomers remember well. UNICEF stands for United Nations International Children's Emergency Fund; its name has been shortened to United Nations Children's Fund, but the old initials are still used. Begun in 1946, UNICEF originally emphasized emergency food aid to international children in crisis, but over the years it has broadened its concerns to include long-term programs and many forms of child protection and advocacy. In 1950 a small group of Presbyterian children in Philadelphia collected change for UNICEF as they went door to door on Halloween, and they sent their fundraising total of $17 to the national UNICEF office.

Thinking this a good idea, in 1953 the United States committee began officially promoting trick-or-treating for UNICEF as a program, and by the next decade millions of children and teenagers were carrying their little Halloween-decorated milk cartons from home to home every year, collecting pocket change for the world's children. Schools and churches played central roles in organizing the campaign in each community. In 1965 UNICEF received the Nobel Peace Prize, and in 1967 President Lyndon Johnson proclaimed that Halloween was UNICEF Day.[24] In over sixty years the United States Fund for UNICEF has raised more than $170 million in its trick-or-treat program; a Canadian version has raised over $96 million. Collections in recent decades have declined dramatically, for a long list of reasons, including political controversies surrounding the United Nations in general and safety concerns about children trick-or-treating for money. The diminished program continues today, although with more emphasis on online donations and fundraising within schools, rather than on door-to-door solicitations.

The children's custom eventually encountered some challenges, from scares about safety and from conservative Christian opposition. Widespread fear about the safety of Halloween treats appeared especially in the 1970s, arising from stories about children being poisoned or hurt by needles inserted into candy or apples. Much of the subsequent study of these

Children bobbing for apples at a Halloween party, c. 1940.

incidents has concluded that the fears were blown out of proportion and most cases were hoaxes or could be explained in other ways. In 1970 a boy from Detroit was reported to have died from heroin inserted into his Halloween candy, but later investigation found that he had discovered the heroin in a relative's home. In 1974 a boy in Texas died from eating candy contaminated with cyanide, but it was determined later that his father had poisoned the boy's candy after taking out a life insurance policy on him. A few additional deaths that were thought to have resulted from eating tampered Halloween candy turned out to be from natural causes. Joel Best, a professor of sociology at the University of Delaware, has tracked newspaper accounts and medical

Halloween

literature about such incidents from 1958 until today. He has found remarkably few examples of real harm to children from tampered treats, and those few often involved detection before any injury occurred. In some of those cases, there are suspicions that the child in question, or a sibling or friend, might have done the tampering to get attention or as a joke. Best concluded, "In my own research, I have been unable to find a substantiated report of a child being killed or seriously injured by a contaminated treat picked up in the course of trick-or-treating." He acknowledges that "one cannot prove a negative," so he can "never prove that no child has been killed by a Halloween sadist," but he has found no such evidence. The hysteria has subsided in recent years, replaced by reasonable concern and due caution, but Best suggests that statistics point to other concerns that merit as much or more attention, like child-pedestrian fatalities from being hit by a car on Halloween night.[25] It remains wise to think about safety in general, but concerns about Halloween dangers should be kept in perspective.

A second challenge has come from the disapproval of conservative Christians. While a segment of Christians opposed Halloween all along, disapproval became especially pronounced after World War II, when Halloween activities centered on children trick-or-treating and the debate was framed as whether Christian parents should allow impressionable children to participate. The question lingers for them even today. Conservative Christians argued that because Halloween was derived from the Celtic Samhain, it was inextricably intertwined with Devil worship and with non-Christian practices and beliefs such as magic, sorcery, witches, ghosts, and evil spirits. In their view, even if modern Halloween practices had changed from those early roots, Halloween was not neutral because it retained underlying associations that mimicked evil practices and tempted children with exposure to the dark side. Conservative Christian responses ranged from total nonparticipation to the creation of alternative Christian activities and, going even further, to making Halloween an occasion for evangelism. One alternative that arose was church-sponsored harvest festivals, with candy, food, games, and wholesome costumes. A similar practice was "trunk or treat," where parents brought their cars to a large parking lot, opened the trunks or pickup tailgates, and distributed candy to children from the backs of their decorated vehicles (trunk or treat also emphasized nonscary costumes). These alternatives attempted to address both safety concerns and inappropriate themes or images. To evangelize, some Christians dropped religious tracts into the candy sacks of trick-or-treaters, and church youth groups organized "hell houses," a conservative Christian alternative to haunted houses that portrayed young people suffering from evils such as abortion, sexual activity, and chemical abuse, along with horrifying glimpses of hell and enticing views of heaven, and a prayer room at the end.

Other Christians came to the defense of Halloween, arguing that almost all holidays have some pre-Christian predecessors, that encounters with scary stories, fear, and even death are natural parts of human development, that Halloween is associated with All Saints' Day, and that it is basically innocent fun. The debate is similar to controversies that arose about the popular Harry Potter books and the alleged dangers of witchcraft, with so many books and articles published by Christians on both sides of the debate that the publications almost became a cottage industry. Yet the general population continued to embrace both Halloween and Harry Potter with enthusiasm, apparently untouched (or perhaps mildly amused) by the sideshow of arguments from Christian conservatives.

ADULT HALLOWEEN

Even in the face of these challenges, the custom of children trick-or-treating continues as a central Halloween ritual to this day, but since the 1970s something has changed. Halloween is no longer about children only. Adults have reentered the party, not replacing children's activities but adding their own festivities.

John Carpenter's 1978 movie played a role. Horror and vampire movies featuring Dracula or Frankenstein or zombies had been popular at Halloween, but the very title of this movie was *Halloween*. The movie takes place on Halloween night, when Michael Myers, who murdered his sister on Halloween fifteen years earlier, breaks out of a sanitarium and terrorizes teenagers, including Jamie Lee Curtis in her first starring role of a long career. The movie was filmed in twenty-one days, on a budget of only $325,000, with handmade props and many actors simply wearing their own clothes, but box office sales totaled $47 million in the United States and $70 million worldwide. The film gave birth to a franchise, with seven sequels, two remakes, and a documentary, plus novels, video games, t-shirts, action figures, and of course masks replicating the frightening pale bluish-white one Michael Myers always wore. *Halloween*'s success helped launch at least two other horror movie series, *Friday the 13th*, featuring Jason (eleven sequels and a remake), and *Nightmare on Elm Street*, with Freddy Krueger (seven sequels and a remake), plus countless other films, some gory, some frightening, some spoofs. *Halloween* is one of the films selected for the United States Film Registry by the Library of Congress, and the summary paragraph comments that "although the numerous imitations and elements of the genre are now considered a cliché," this film that started it is "uniquely artistic, frightening and a horror film keystone."[26]

The very name of the original, *Halloween*, not only identified the night on which its events took place but also firmly located the Halloween holiday as a proper home for the horror movie genres. In a nod to Halloween's origins, the plot of *Halloween III: Season of the Witch* (the only sequel directed by Carpenter and the only one that did not include the Michael Myers character) involved a plot to resurrect the Celtic Samhain festival. What is important here is that the primary audience for these horror films was young adults; it certainly was not children. Teenagers made these films popular. The surprise success of this low-budget movie and its successors can be explained at least partially by the desire of young adults to be included in Halloween festivities. From their perspective, this was a night for pretending and experimenting, for some release from societal inhibitions, and for playing with adult themes of fear and death, all of which was missing from a sanitized children's costume parade. The movies helped add young adult participation back into Halloween.

There have been many other indications of what one journalist called "the adultification of Halloween" since the 1970s, including parades, haunted houses, specialized Halloween stores, house decorations, and costume parties in bars, concert venues, and homes, for grownups of many ages. More and more adults decorate the outside of their homes at Halloween, not just to scare or entertain trick-or-treaters but in acknowledgment of the season. Some of the displays are so lavish they rival Christmas decorations. The Knott's Berry Farm amusement park in Southern California becomes Knott's Scary Farm for a month prior to Halloween. The West Hollywood Halloween costume carnival draws half a million spectators and is second only to Pasadena's Rose Bowl Parade as the largest annual event in the Los Angeles area. Spirit Halloween specialty stores were founded in 1983 "out of the observation of a trend on the verge of explosion" and were acquired by Spencer Gifts in 1999. By 2014 the company was opening more than 1,100 temporary stores between Labor Day and Halloween, offering "the most comprehensive one-stop destinations for everything shoppers can imagine for Halloween." An estimated 3,000 temporary haunted houses open throughout the nation for Halloween, often with age limits to restrict the attendance of young children.[27] The list of examples of ways in which Halloween has become an adult holiday is long. Consider three more illustrations: parades, beer marketing, and sexy costumes.

The most notable Halloween parade began in 1974, when puppeteer Ralph Lee and others founded the Village Halloween Parade in New York City's Greenwich Village, with giant puppets, outrageous costumes, bands, and huge crowds. This parade is far different from the family-oriented parades in Anoka, Minnesota. Anyone with a costume is allowed to march the mile-long route, and over the years the parade has grown to an estimated 60,000 annual marchers and spectators in the millions. In 2011 the *New York Daily News* reported that "the costumes ran the full gamut, from the spectacular to the scary, the perverted to the perverse, the bawdy to the downright bizarre." One participant remarked, "This is all-inclusive, 'cause everyone wants to get their freak flag on tonight."[28] Although the parade had to be canceled in 2012 because of Superstorm Sandy, it continues, and it probably remains the largest and wildest of the American Halloween parades. The New York parade and others in Los Angeles (West Hollywood), New Orleans, Key West, Vancouver, and elsewhere have featured significant percentages of gay marchers, just one example of the diversity of the participants.

Coors Brewing Company embraced Halloween when it developed campaigns to market its product as the "official beer of Halloween." For three years in the 1980s, the company's television commercials featured the seductive character Elvira, played by actress Cassandra Peterson. Clad in a gothic black dress and displaying significant cleavage, Elvira once introduced horror movies on a Los Angeles television station; through national syndication, she became a widely recognized celebrity. Store displays of Coors Light included life-size cardboard stand-ups of Elvira that were frequently stolen by admirers. Elvira became known as the Queen of Halloween, and sales of Coors beer soared. "How sad to have a holiday you love so much and then grow out of it," Peterson has remarked. "I do have to take some credit for Halloween becoming an adult holiday."[29]

Elvira's iconic image raises a further aspect of the adult Halloween, costumes. Halloween is one of the fastest-growing holidays for consumer spending; in 2014, the National Retail Federation's annual consumer spending survey indicated that Americans would spend $7.4 billion for Halloween. Of this, $2.8 billion, or 38 percent, was for costumes. (The other two major

Halloween expenditures are candy at $2.2 billion and decorations at $2 billion.) Subdivided, $1.1 billion was for children's costumes, but even more—$1.4 billion—was for adults. There was even $350 million budgeted for pet costumes! Two-thirds of all American adults planned to celebrate Halloween, and about half of those intended to dress in costume; more than a third intended to throw or attend a party. And if there is any doubt that this is adult activity, a perusal of print advertisements for Halloween costumes or a glance around the room at a Halloween party will confirm that a significant proportion of the costumes are suggestive or sexy. As Lindsay Lohan's character said in the movie *Mean Girls*, Halloween is "the one night of the year when you can dress like a slut and no other girls can say anything about it."

Recently, a claim that Halloween has become the second most commercialized holiday in the United States has been cropping up repeatedly. I have been unable to track down where the claim originated, but it simply is not true. If we compare holiday spending, Christmas is first, of course. But at least according to statistics provided by the National Retail Federation, several other holidays rank above Halloween for annual consumer purchases, including Mother's Day, Valentine's Day (with all of those engagement rings), Easter, Father's Day, and even the Super Bowl. Even so, the amount of spending for Halloween is indeed substantial and has increased by more than 55 percent in the past decade. An accurate statement might be that Halloween is one of the *fastest growing* holidays for consumer spending in the United States.[30]

So why is Halloween so popular? How did it grow from an early Celtic observance to national American celebration and then, in the past few decades, to cultural and commercial juggernaut? Among many contributing factors, I would argue that two are especially important.

The first is that it is a holiday unfettered by much religious or national meaning. For almost all participants, except for a neo-pagan minority, Halloween contains no call to recommit to anything. Christmas and Easter remind Christians to recommit themselves to religious meanings about the birth, death, and resurrection of Jesus, even if other cultural aspects also are attached to the days. Valentine's Day emphasizes a recommitment or new commitment to relationships, whether with romantic partners or family and friends. Thanksgiving involves an implied recommitment to family, nation, and/or God, as it encourages participants to appreciate and give thanks for their blessings. In the case of Halloween, yes, an overlay of Christian meaning was provided when All Saints' Day moved into the general time period on November 1, but Halloween's festivities became concentrated on the night before, and the serious religious messages were reserved for the next two days. That freed Halloween to be primarily an occasion for letting go, much like Mardi Gras prior to Lent. Very few people issue admonitions to remember the deeper meanings of the evening. It is a time of release, a rare opportunity for reduced inhibitions and fun. Tim Burton, the noted film director and producer and co-writer of *The Nightmare before Christmas*, summarized the spirit of Halloween very well: "To me, Hallowe'en has always been the most fun night of the year. It's where rules are dropped and you can be anything at all. Fantasy rules. It's only scary in a funny way. Nobody's out to really scare anybody to death. They're out to delight people with their scariness, which is what Hallowe'en is all about."[31]

Costumes provide a chance to pretend to be someone else, to wear clothing never worn on ordinary days, to inhabit the imagination, to party and play. A number of theorists have written about the need for these opportunities in human lives, the need to at least temporarily overturn some of the norms of daily life and release antisocial impulses. The result might reinforce society's status quo by giving people a chance to vent some urges for a limited time, and/or it might be liberating, opening participants to new possibilities. With so many other holidays restrained by their calls to deeper meanings, to recommitment, Halloween is the only one of the five holidays examined here that focuses on release.

The second significant factor in explaining Halloween's recent rise in popularity is sheer numbers. Baby boomers, including me, remember our childhood experiences trick-or-treating and wonder why Halloween's popularity has expanded so much since then. The answer is simple. When we were children, Halloween was mostly about children. Since then, both young adults and older adults have joined the party, which has more than doubled the number of participants. Adults now spend more money on their own costumes than on children's costumes, and it is adults who have invested more in yard decorations and party preparations. Children's activities continue, but adults have been added. The audience is bigger, and the adults have more money to spend. It is not hard to do the math.

One other note. Anyone who is aware of Mexico's Day of the Dead (Dia de los Muertos) will notice striking similarities between that day and Halloween in the United States. The two are quite distinct but also related, in a way that illustrates the metaphor of the three-layer cake described in this book's first chapter. Let me explain.

Long before Spaniards entered what is now Mexico and portions of Central and South America, Aztec, Mayan, and other indigenous people celebrated days of the dead, sometimes in early or late summer. When Spaniards conquered the region they brought with them Catholicism, including the observance of All Saints' Day and All Souls' Day on November 1 and 2. Because the Spaniards sought to eliminate native beliefs and practices and replace them with Christianity, some scholars believe that the natives moved their Day of the Dead to November 1 so that they could continue their previous rituals under the guise of the new Christian holy days. One Christian missionary stated this directly, writing that the Aztec Day of the Dead had been "passed to the Feast of Allhallows in order to cover up the ancient ceremony."[32] So some aspects of the day are Catholic beliefs and rituals, but it also is shaped by earlier indigenous traditions.

What has resulted varies from region to region in Mexico and in surrounding areas, but common practices include building altars and visiting graves to remember and pray for those who have died and to spend time with the souls of the departed. Altars are built in homes and cemeteries and decorated with pictures of the deceased, samples of their favorite food and drink, toys for children, sugar skulls, and marigolds to attract the souls of the dead. Visits to cemeteries might include eating a meal with the departed and sharing news and remembrances. Generally, what is different from Halloween is that the Day of the Dead is not an especially scary or fearful time. Death is seen as an essential part of life, and there is comfort in spending time with the souls of the deceased, and room for humor and even irreverence. It is a family-oriented time honoring the dead. Symbolically, it is a time for dancing with skeletons instead of running away from them.

In terms of the three-layer cake, Halloween and the Day of the Dead have different pre-Christian roots, one arising out of a Celtic background and the other arising out of Aztec and associated Mesoamerican rituals for the dead. Their first layers are very dissimilar, although both admittedly pertain to death in some way. However, they share the same second layer—Christianity, which entered both regions and introduced the observance of All Saints' Day on November 1. The result is two holidays that share similar dates, a Catholic influence, and some attention to the dead. Yet they are distinct, with different symbols, practices, and general themes, and obviously one reason for the differences is the influence of their Celtic or Mesoamerican roots. When it comes to the third layer, the influence of modern popular culture, a major question is how much these two observances will influence one another in the future. Aspects of the American Halloween have been exported to many parts of the world, including neighboring Mexico, much to the consternation of those who want to protect the Day of the Dead as an important Mexican national tradition not to be undermined by foreign influences. The growing Hispanic population in the United States also brings both holidays into direct contact with one another. In the coming decades, will they remain separate, or will one eclipse the other, or will they blend together? Stay tuned.

Thanksgiving

Every American, especially anyone who has ever attended public school, knows about the first Thanksgiving. In 1620 the *Mayflower* sailed from England with 102 passengers and landed at Plymouth Rock, to found a colony in the New World. Their first winter was very difficult and about half of them died. In the spring they received help from a Native American, Squanto, who showed them how to grow crops in this new land, and in the fall after the harvest they decided to give thanks to God for their blessings and to celebrate by

The First Thanksgiving of the Pilgrims, 1621. After a painting by Jean Leon Gerome Ferris.

inviting Indians in the area to join them for a meal. That was the first Thanksgiving, in 1621, and that is why we have a national holiday each fall, to remember our Pilgrim beginnings and to give thanks. Correct?

Yes and no. At several points, no. It's complicated.

A study of how Thanksgiving came to be is fascinating, not only to learn what is historical and what is not, but to see the shifts and additions along the way.

PURITAN BEGINNINGS

At first glance the American Thanksgiving seems to merge two traditions or themes: days of thanksgiving and harvest celebrations. However, in their historical roots the two did not necessarily arise together, so to understand how the holiday developed in the United States we should consider each one separately. To begin, for the moment set aside all thoughts about the fall season and harvests and consider instead a tradition of thanksgiving days that could happen at any time of the year. Ironically, and I cannot overstate the irony, it was the Puritans, the very people who opposed annual celebrations of Christmas and Easter, who brought days of thanksgiving from England to America.

Puritans were mentioned briefly in the chapters on Christmas and Easter, but this is the place to say a bit more about who the Puritans were and what they thought about holidays. Prior to the early 1500s, England was officially Roman Catholic. The story about Henry VIII is fairly well known: Henry wanted Pope Clement VII to annul his marriage to Catherine of Aragon so that he could marry Anne Boleyn, and the pope refused. Of course, as with most historical events, the story is more complicated than that, but the result was that Henry and parliament broke from the Catholic Church and formed the Church of England. It was mainly an institutional break, with the king replacing the pope as head of the church in England, but in many other ways the Church of England continued Catholic beliefs and practices, simply with new leadership. Some dissenters known as Puritans were influenced by the theology of Protestant reformer John Calvin, and they believed that the Church of England did not go far enough in eliminating Roman Catholic elements that, in their view, were not based in scripture.

One major target was the year-round ritual calendar that included Christmas, Easter, many saints' days, and more. The popular conception of Puritans has been influenced by remarks such as H. L. Mencken's, who wrote that Puritanism was "the haunting fear that someone, somewhere, may be happy."[1] Puritan opposition to these holidays may seem to fit this dour image, but there were some understandable reasons for the Puritans' uneasiness about holidays, and they were shared by others. Prior to Henry VIII, England observed 147 religious holidays throughout the year, including Sundays. That might sound good, because they were days off work, but they were also days without pay, and church attendance was mandatory. The huge number of special days interfered with the general economy and the completion of vital tasks such as harvests. So much idle time also provided occasions for troublesome public behavior. For both practical and religious reasons, in 1536 Henry VIII reduced the number of festival days other than Sundays to twenty-seven, but for some Puritans that still left too many. They argued that Sundays were enough, that the vital Christian themes were lifted up on Sundays, and that all other holy days were unjustified Catholic additions.

However, Puritans did participate in occasional days of fasting and days of thanksgiving, sometimes declared by the Church of England but developed even further by the Puritans. What was different about these days is that they were not annual observances that took place on the same date each year. They took place only when events warranted. A day of thanksgiving might be declared to celebrate and thank God for a particular military victory, or good health following a wave of disease, or an especially bountiful harvest that saved people from starvation. On the other hand, days of humiliation and fasting were declared in response to negative happenings, such as droughts, fires, or military defeats; in those cases, Puritans would pray to discern their sins, to repent, and to ask for God's assistance and blessing. Both kinds of days were serious religious events. They involved attendance at a special worship service in the morning, and sometimes in the afternoon as well, followed by a family meal later in the day, where the especially pious would continue their reflection on the scripture passages and sermons heard earlier. So when Puritans established colonies in New England, they brought with them a ritual calendar consisting only of Sundays, but they also brought the practice of occasional days of fasting or thanksgiving, sometimes called Providential holidays, that might arise for specific reasons in some years.[2]

By the way, this entire background applies to both Puritans and Pilgrims in the New World. Really, they were all Puritans. The difference was between what we might call separating Puritans and nonseparating Puritans. The separating Puritans (also called Separatists) gave up hoping that the Church of England would ever make the changes they wanted, and many fled to the Netherlands. They were among those who traveled on the legendary *Mayflower*, landing in 1620 at the location that would become Plymouth, Massachusetts, soon led by William Bradford. In at least one of Bradford's manuscripts he called the settlers "saints" and "pilgrimes," but the term "Pilgrim" did not become widely used until more than a century later, in the late 1700s.[3] The other Puritans, not separatist, made additional efforts to change the Church of England, but some of them also were drawn to the New World as an experiment to put their beliefs into practice, and they were instrumental in establishing the Massachusetts Bay Colony (1629) and the Colony of Connecticut (1636). Puritans also were active in what became New Hampshire, and Puritan dissenters from Massachusetts were involved in establishing Rhode Island. Thus, Pilgrims were a subgroup of the larger group called Puritans; they were the separating Puritans who founded Plymouth.

And notice the geographical locations of the colonies mentioned here, separatist or not. References to America's Puritan beginnings mainly involve the northern section of the thirteen colonies—Puritan New England—and not the entire colonial enterprise all along the East Coast.

Although there might have been prior examples, the earliest fast day in New England that can be documented was in Plymouth Colony in the summer of 1623, and it was in response to a drought. Miracle of miracles, following the day of prayers it began to rain the very next morning. The rain continued for several days, and Governor Bradford declared a day of thanksgiving shortly thereafter. Massachusetts Bay colonists brought similar practices when they arrived in 1630; the same was true of the Connecticut and New Haven colonies, less so in Rhode Island. Fasts and thanksgivings for particular occasions could be declared by either church or civil authorities, and they were common throughout the 1600s.

However, there is an understandable human impulse in the late fall to celebrate after the work of a harvest is over, food has been stored for the winter, and time is available for reflection on the blessings and struggles of the past year. The Puritans were not immune to this impulse. In the 1640s, civil leaders in Connecticut farming towns began to declare annual fall days of thanksgiving, a regular observance on the same date every year, and the practice arose in other New England colonies as well. Some ministers were opposed to this innovation. They believed that the traditional observance of particular days gave proper attention to God, and they feared that annual observances would cause people to take blessings for granted and the days would lose their meaning. Nevertheless, the annual fall celebrations were popular, and colonists began to expect them. By the early 1700s annual official days of thanksgiving had been declared by the governors of Connecticut, Massachusetts, and New Hampshire, although not on the same dates. These thanksgiving days tended to be in late November or early December, usually on a Thursday. It was important that they be held in the middle of the week, to assure that they did not interfere with or replace Sunday observances. The annual days very late in the fall were a time for general assessment and thanksgiving as the Puritans entered the winter season, and harvest was only part of it; after all, most harvests had been completed much earlier than late November. This is an important point. For the northern portion of North America, where seasons change more dramatically, the timing of Halloween is more appropriate for a harvest festival than Thanksgiving is. Thanksgiving, if it is partially a harvest festival, is a very belated one.

The annual days of thanksgiving consisted mainly of worship services and family dinners, and as this was repeated over the years, the colonists came to assume they had always celebrated that way. In fact, remembering that Puritans were opposed to Christmas, historian James Baker has suggested that "Thanksgiving took the place of Christmas in New England, acting as a seasonal break of meeting and feasting before the worst winter weather and gloomy days set in." For New England Puritans, "Thanksgiving was the major early winter holiday."[4] By the time of the American Revolution, the tradition of an annual late-fall thanksgiving was well under way in New England, alongside the continuing practice of declaring particular days for fasts or thanksgiving. Because the Church of England also had engaged in specific days of fasting and thanksgiving back in the home country, other American colonies south of New England, where the Church of England was more prominent, likewise proclaimed days of thanksgiving for particular reasons, but they had very little of the annual fall tradition.

The Continental Congress, and the new nation that followed, enacted some national days of thanksgiving, most often of the particular kind. The first national Thanksgiving Day declared by the Continental Congress was December 18, 1777. It was to give thanks for the defeat of the British army at Saratoga, New York, a surprising and significant victory for the unseasoned colonial troops under the leadership of Benedict Arnold (the same person who later defected to the British and whose name became a synonym for traitor). While a military victory was the specific reason for the special day, Samuel Adams of Massachusetts wrote the proclamation, and because of his New England background the document included general themes that sounded "very like a traditional proclamation for New England's annual holiday."[5] The next year, the Continental Congress declared a thanksgiving day for December 30, 1778, in gratitude for a treaty alliance with France supporting the American Revolution. This is interesting, because the agreement with the French happened in the spring, but the designated date to give thanks for it was in December. It seems to represent the combination of the two kinds of thanksgiving, merging thanksgivings for a particular reason with the New England tradition of an annual thanksgiving celebration on a Thursday in late fall. The Continental Congress continued proclaiming a day of thanksgiving each year for some specific reason associated with the war, but always on a Thursday in late fall. After the Treaty of Paris concluded the Revolutionary War, the Continental Congress declared thanksgiving days for December 11, 1783, and October 19, 1784, in gratitude for peace. These were the last of eight annual fall proclamations of thanksgiving days. Then, with the war over and with other colonies complaining that a New England tradition was being forced upon them, thanksgiving proclamations by the Continental Congress ended.

In the new United States, each president handled thanksgiving days differently. George Washington proclaimed two days of thanksgiving during his presidency, the first on November 26, 1789, to celebrate the adoption of the United States Constitution. The idea of declaring a national day was controversial in the first United States Congress. Opponents argued that some citizens resented the new constitution, that two states had not yet ratified it, and that thanksgiving proclamations should be left to the states and were not a matter for federal action. In addition, Thomas Tucker of South Carolina argued that thanksgiving "is a religious matter, and as such it is proscribed to us," in other words, not appropriate for involvement by the federal government.[6] These arguments represented a political struggle between Federalists, who supported a strong central government and saw a role for religion in undergirding the social order, and Anti-Federalists, who feared tyranny from a too-powerful central government and who were similarly nervous about the influence of church hierarchies. In this instance the Federalists won. Washington proclaimed one other day of thanksgiving during his presidency, February 19, 1795, to celebrate his ability to put down the Whiskey Rebellion and to stay neutral in a war then raging in Europe. Note that the date of this particular day of thanksgiving was not in the fall but in February. In fact it got Washington in trouble with churches that observed Lent, because this thanksgiving fell the day after Ash Wednesday, creating a celebration that interrupted what was supposed to be a somber period of repentance leading up to Easter.

John Adams, the next president, proclaimed no national days of thanksgiving. Some historians have mistakenly claimed he declared two, in 1798 and 1799, but they actually were announced as the other kind of special day, days of fasting and prayer as the United States struggled to avoid war with France. The next two presidents, Thomas Jefferson and James Madison, Anti-Federalists, had been principal architects of the clause in the constitutional First Amendment protecting religious freedom and resisting government interference. As a result, both took the issue of thanksgiving proclamations very seriously. Jefferson believed that the president had "no authority to direct the religious exercises of his constituents" and issued no such proclamations.[7] Madison decided that nationally proclaimed days of fasting or thanksgiving could be appropriate only if they were limited to recommendations, with no requirements to attend worship, and if they were extended to all Christian denominations and all non-Christian religions equally. With those understandings, he declared three days of fasting and prayer during the War of 1812, and one day of thanksgiving, April 13, 1815, for the conclusion of the conflict. After that, there were no more presidential thanksgiving proclamations for the next forty-eight years.

A NATIONAL HOLIDAY

Thanksgiving eventually became a national holiday mainly because of two influences: the diffusion of New Englanders throughout the United States, and the tireless advocacy of one remarkable, very persistent magazine editor.

The fabled story of the American West, with easterners moving from the settled Atlantic coast to new opportunities on the frontier, included its share of New Englanders. They settled in neighboring areas like western New York State, Pennsylvania, and Ohio, and later in Michigan, Wisconsin, Iowa, Indiana, and Illinois, in the northern tier of the country. About 800,000 New Englanders moved into this new region from 1790 to 1820, and by 1850 their number was one and a half million.[8] Of course they brought their social institutions with them, including Thanksgiving. In Wisconsin, for example, the editor of the *Milwaukee Sentinel* wrote in 1838, "Why can't we have a Thanksgiving out West here as we used to in good old New England? We do wish the governor would think of this thing."[9] The governor did, proclaiming the first Thanksgiving in Wisconsin in 1839.

New Englanders spread throughout other sections of the nation as well, in the south and in western territories. Even when they did not make up a large part of the population, they often were persons of influence, like teachers, editors, and ministers. Although these New Englanders did not mount a coordinated campaign for a nationwide Thanksgiving, their influence helped encourage other states to adopt the tradition.

In Sarah Josepha Buell Hale the movement for a national day of thanksgiving found a leader. She is not a household name among Americans today, but if anyone has heard of her it is probably because of her role in the adoption of Thanksgiving as a national holiday. She was an extraordinary woman, and a brief review of her life helps explain her influence. Hale (1788–1879) was born in New Hampshire (yes, in New England) to parents who believed in the full education of both boys and girls, in a day when fewer girls had a chance to attend school. Educated by her mother at home, she read from literature like the Bible, John Bunyan's *Pilgrim's Progress*, and the works of Milton, Johnson, Burns, and Shakespeare. She also learned from her brother, who attended Dartmouth College. She became a teacher when she was eighteen, and when she married lawyer David Hale at age twenty-five, they studied together for hours each night, on a wide array of subjects, from French to botany. Her husband died young, of pneumonia, just before the birth of their fifth child, and she wore black in mourning for the remainder of her life. But she certainly did not retire from life.

In 1827 she published her first novel, *Northwood: Life North and South*, one of the first American novels about slavery. From there she became editor of *Ladies' Magazine*, which later merged into *Godey's Lady's Book*, the most widely circulated and influential American magazine of its time, for any audience. She edited the magazine for forty years (she preferred to be called the "editress"), influencing fashion, values, household decoration, and politics. In more recent terms, she has been described as "Oprah and Martha Stewart combined."[10] In an era of activism for women's suffrage, she did not support the movement, because she accepted the belief that men and women had separate spheres, but she was a tireless advocate for women's education, including higher education, and helped found Vassar College. She advocated expanding women's roles in the workforce, started what is sometimes credited as being the first day nursery, supported public playgrounds, argued for addressing public health and sanitation problems, helped found the Seaman's Aid Society to benefit the families of men who died at sea, worked to preserve George Washington's home at Mount Vernon, and raised money to finish the Bunker Hill Monument. She also wrote at least two dozen books—or almost fifty, depending on how one counts her collected essays and poems. To top off the list, she is the person who wrote "Mary Had a Little Lamb," which is included in one of her books of poems for children. Hale retired from editing at age 89 in 1877, the same year that Thomas Edison recited the beginning of her poem as the first words recorded for his new invention, the phonograph.

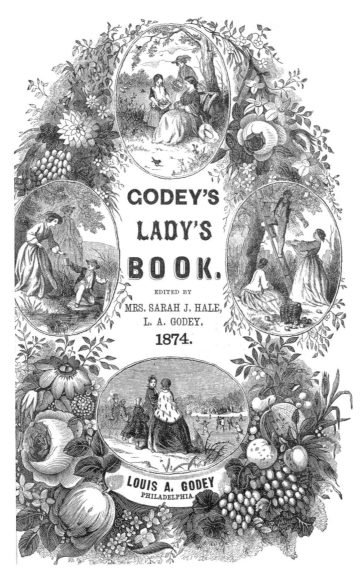

The cover of the July 1874 issue of *Godey's Lady's Book*, the influential magazine edited by Sarah Josepha Hale.

Early on, Hale recommended the Thanksgiving holiday as an example of New England culture and values that should be adopted elsewhere. Her novel *Northwood* included two chapters on the topic, "A Thanksgiving Sermon" and "Thanksgiving Dinner," and at one point in the novel an Englishman asks whether Thanksgiving Day is universally observed in America. The father of the main character replies, "Not yet, but I trust it will become so. We have too few holidays. Thanksgiving, like the Fourth of July, should be considered a national festival, and observed by all our people." In light of the full campaign she would launch two decades later, it is clear that was an exact expression of Hale's views. She believed Thanksgiving should become the nation's third national holiday, alongside Washington's Birthday and Independence Day.

In 1846, with *Godey's Lady's Book* as her base of influence, Hale began writing strongly worded editorials every year promoting Thanksgiving as a national holiday, and the November issues of her magazine were filled with Thanksgiving poems, heartwarming short stories about family gatherings for Thanksgiving dinner, cooking advice, and much more. Hale understood that the first step was to persuade as many states as possible to adopt the holiday, and then a national mandate might follow. She wrote personal letters every year to the governors of every US state and territory, and to the United States president as well. Zachary Taylor, Millard Fillmore, Franklin Pierce, James Buchanan, and Abraham Lincoln all received yearly appeals asking that the last Thursday in November be declared a national holiday, Thanksgiving. A number of Protestant churches joined the campaign, and magazines in addition to *Godey's* added Thanksgiving pictures and stories to the movement.

The bandwagon rolled along, pushed by Sarah Josepha Hale and supported by New Englanders scattered throughout the nation. New York had adopted the holiday in 1817, and Michigan in 1824, but the greatest number of states joined in the 1840s. New Jersey, Pennsylvania, Ohio, Wisconsin, Illinois, and Iowa added Thanksgiving in the 1850s. By 1860, Thanksgiving had been officially proclaimed in thirty states and two territories; territories sometimes declared the holiday even before they received statehood. The Civil War complicated matters, but even then, both the north and the south issued thanksgiving proclamations, although they were of the particular kind, to celebrate military victories.

Abraham Lincoln declared two days of thanksgiving for military triumphs, one on April 13, 1862, and a second on August 6, 1863, the latter for the victory at Gettysburg. However, that same fall Lincoln issued another thanksgiving declaration that was very different from the previous two. It was for the last Thursday in November, just what Sara Hale and others were seeking, and it was a general call for a thanksgiving not tied to any particular battle or event. That proclamation is generally regarded as the beginning of today's American Thanksgiving. Lincoln's proclamation and other writings make no mention of Hale, but many assume she deserves part of the credit for the day. At that time no one knew if it would become an annual tradition, but in the following year, 1864, Lincoln again proclaimed the last Thursday in November as Thanksgiving. Lincoln was assassinated before the next November, but the new president, Andrew Johnson, continued with a Thanksgiving proclamation for 1865, although on a slightly different date, the first Thursday in December. The next year Johnson returned to the previous practice, the last Thursday in November, and presidents continued the tradition every year after that until 1939.

These proclamations were annual traditions not enshrined in law. The general public assumed the holiday would happen every year, but Hale continued campaigning, now for legal status. She wrote in an 1871 editorial,

> But one thing is wanting. It is eminently fit that this National Holiday shall rest upon the same legal basis as its companions, the Twenty-second of February [Washington's birthday] and the Fourth of July. As things now stand, our Thanksgiving is exposed to the chances of the time. Unless the President or the Governor of the State in office happens to see fit, no day is appointed for its observance. Is not this a state of things which calls for instant remedy? Should not our festival be assured to us by law?[11]

"Thanksgiving-Day," illustration by Thomas Nast, 1863, marking President Lincoln's declaring November 26, 1863, the first national day of Thanksgiving.

Hale did not live to see a national Thanksgiving Day attain legal status, but it did happen more than half a century later, which is an interesting story in itself.

In the first year of Franklin Delano Roosevelt's presidency, 1933, November had five Thursdays, and because Thanksgiving's traditional date was the last Thursday, it fell on the very last day of the month, November 30. By that time the commercialized Christmas was well under way and the day after Thanksgiving had emerged as the beginning of most Christmas purchases, so the late Thanksgiving date severely shortened that year's Christmas shopping season. Since Thanksgiving depended on an annual proclamation by the president, who technically could do what he wished, retailers appealed to FDR to move Thanksgiving one week earlier, but he declined. However, in 1939 it happened again. November once again had five Thursdays, and business interests repeated their request. The Great Depression, at its worst back in 1933, still lingered. This time Roosevelt agreed, moving Thanksgiving one week earlier, and a storm of controversy erupted. Calendars had already been printed, school schedules set, football games arranged, family plans made. In terms of days off work, a president's proclamation applied only to federal employees and residents of Washington, DC; for other persons it depended on the actions of each state's governor. In a political climate of very divided opinions about FDR, twenty-three states accepted the new date, twenty-three states retained the traditional one, and two states (Colorado and Texas) observed both dates. The Republican mayor of Atlantic City, Charles White, called the earlier date "Franksgiving," a term that caught on with critics. Alf Landon, the Republican presidential candidate who had lost to FDR in 1936, said that Roosevelt had announced the changed Thanksgiving date "to an unprepared country with the omnipotence of a Hitler."[12] The classic movie *Holiday Inn* (1942), in which Irving Berlin's song "White Christmas" was first heard, included an animated sequence in which a bewildered cartoon turkey moved between two dates on the page of a calendar, an obvious reference to the then-recent controversy. Indeed, one can imagine the complications for an extended family in which members crossed state lines to gather for a Thanksgiving dinner if each state recognized a different date. The confusion continued for two more years, although some additional states accepted the earlier date in 1940 and 1941. Finally, in December 1941 Congress passed and FDR signed legislation declaring the *fourth* Thursday of November to be the official national date of Thanksgiving. It was an effective compromise, because in most years it would be the traditional last Thursday of the month, but in years with five Thursdays, having Thanksgiving on the fourth Thursday assured a substantial Christmas shopping season. The bottom line is that the date of Thanksgiving was clarified and finally made legal mainly for economic reasons.

THE SURPRISE

So Thanksgiving became a national holiday, first through annual presidential proclamations that began with Abraham Lincoln, and much later through congressional action. But here is the big surprise. Throughout the entire campaign just described, by New Englanders, Hale, churches, and official state and presidential proclamations, almost no one referred to Pilgrims' and Indians' having gathered to give thanks in Plymouth in 1621, because they did not know about it. The story that is now considered the central Thanksgiving narrative for Americans was not what promoters had in mind when they championed the cause to make Thanksgiving a national holiday. In other words, the national holiday came first, and the Pilgrim and Indian story was filled in later.

When nonfiction author Penny Colman personally encountered questions about the Pilgrim and Indian Thanksgiving that she and most of the rest of us learned about in childhood, she decided to read everything Sarah Josepha Hale wrote about Thanksgiving. She reported that up to the Lincoln proclamation, Hale never wrote about the 1621 story. Ever. In Hale's *North-*

wood novel one character said that Thanksgiving began in 1631 in Boston, when a ship arrived to save the colonists from starvation. In one of her *Godey's* editorials Hale said essentially the same thing: "To the Colony of Massachusetts belongs the honor of introducing this holiday, soon after the settlement of Boston. . . . From that Colony the observance of Thanksgiving became the custom in all New England, then advanced slowly but steadily on to the Middle States and the West." Other than that, she made almost no historical references at all. The reason is that her focus was not on nostalgia or looking back, but on giving thanks for blessings in the present and on uniting the nation, which became even more important during and after the Civil War. Thanksgiving Day, revolving around worship and the family dinner, would "awaken in American hearts the love of home and country, of thankfulness to God, and peace between brethren," uniting all Americans as "one Great Family Republic."[13]

Another historian found the same absence in earlier official proclamations. Robert Tracy McKenzie reported that "out of 223 colonial or state proclamations I have located from the years 1676–1840, *not a single one* refers to the Pilgrims, even euphemistically." None of the presidential proclamations explicitly referred to Pilgrims until FDR's declaration of 1939, when he changed the date of Thanksgiving.[14] The 1621 Pilgrim and Indian story also cannot be found in most magazine and newspaper articles about Thanksgiving from the 1800s, or in most books or magazines for children of the time. When history was mentioned, it was agreed that Thanksgiving started in New England, and the most common specific incidents cited were the 1623 relief from drought in Plymouth and the 1631 arrival of supplies in Boston, but there was virtually nothing about a 1621 event with Pilgrims and Indians.

Early historical considerations of American Puritanism focused on Massachusetts Bay and Boston, seeing Plymouth only as a small early part of the larger wave of Puritan immigration. In 1720, no group commemorated the centennial anniversary of the 1620 Plymouth landing. Activities of remembrance and commemoration began to develop in the mid-1700s, and later in the century the term "Pilgrim" became an increasingly common label for the early Plymouth settlers. By the bicentennial anniversary of the Plymouth landing in 1820, a newly organized Plymouth Society sponsored a commemoration featuring the famous and influential senator Daniel Webster, who delivered what has been called the "Plymouth Oration," one of the classic speeches in American history. Webster employed the phrase "Pilgrim Fathers" repeatedly and lifted them up for homage, praising them for providing an inheritance of virtue, piety, and civic principles. Key historical documents were rediscovered in the early and middle 1800s, including an account of the now famous 1621 thanksgiving, although the details of that first thanksgiving did not immediately become widespread knowledge. Henry Wadsworth Longfellow's popular *Courtship of Miles Standish* (1858) added a legend about romance to the gradually growing public interest in the Plymouth colonists, by now called Pilgrims. For all of these reasons, public awareness of Plymouth grew throughout the century. By the end of the 1800s and the early 1900s, a number of novels, illustrations, and histories for children and adults told the story of the Plymouth beginnings, including a 1621 thanksgiving gathering of Pilgrims and Indians, which was about to become the dominant Thanksgiving story.

One complication is that once a national Thanksgiving Day was established, several locations eventually claimed that theirs was the first thanksgiving. In addition to the idea that the first such celebration occurred in Boston in 1630 or 1631, at least ten other claims have been made for the first thanksgiving, from 1513 to 1619 and in locations from Florida and Texas to Virginia and Maine. Some were simply a Mass or a worship service, sometimes with a feast, and two were celebrated with Native Americans.[15] Some of the claims arose only in later years.

The story of the thanksgiving in Plymouth in 1621 became the predominant one because it fit with the previous assumption that Thanksgiving began in

New England, and the overall Plymouth experience was emerging in the 1800s as *the* symbolic foundational national story, one highlighting the settlers' ocean voyage and the Mayflower Compact. Appearing somewhat separate from the other Puritans, the Pilgrims could be portrayed as a more appealing example for the national mythology than the strict, witch-burning Massachusetts Bay colonists. The story of the Pilgrim thanksgiving gathering was frosting on the cake, a welcome addition to the Plymouth narrative.

Public schools in particular seized upon the story and made the shared meal, featuring Pilgrims with buckles on their shoes and Indians with war bonnets, a part of every schoolchild's memories. After about 1890, public schools began giving added attention to national holidays in general, as a means of teaching American history and instilling principles of civic virtue and patriotism. This task was considered even more urgent because of the massive immigration of Europeans from many nations who poured into the United States following the Civil War and, leaders believed, needed to be properly Americanized. The cycle of American holidays included Washington's Birthday, Lincoln's Birthday, Memorial Day, Flag Day, and Independence Day, and all except the last fell within the school year. Among them, Thanksgiving Day played a vital role.

Standard school history books now included the 1621 story, volumes like Margaret Pumphrey's *Stories of the Pilgrims* (1910) appeared, and school supply companies provided iconic images of Pilgrims and Indians for school decoration and instruction. A common school practice was the Thanksgiving pageant, with schoolchildren playing the parts of Pilgrims and Indians. As described in one newspaper article, "There are little boys in high cardboard hats and silver cardboard buckles. Little girls trip on long gray skirts. And the Indians in crepe paper say, majestically, 'Me Massasoit, me great chief,' or, less impressively, 'Me Squanto, me friendly.'"[16]

As it developed, the 1621 Pilgrim and Indian story also included stereotypes, caricatures, and legendary additions. How much do we know about

Schoolchildren in Pilgrim costumes, 1935.

the event's actual history? Very little. The only direct description we have is from a letter written by Edward Winslow to a friend in England on December 12, 1621. Winslow was a Separatist Puritan who traveled on the *Mayflower* in 1620 and was a key leader who assisted Governor Bradford in the new colony. In 1646, he returned to England to work eventually in the government of Oliver Cromwell, leader of England's Puritan Revolution, and never returned to Plymouth. The following paragraph from Winslow's letter is the only narrative we have of what happened in the fall of 1621:

> Our harvest being gotten in, our governor sent four men on fowling, that so we might after a special manner rejoice together, after we had gathered the fruits of our labors; they four in one day killed as much fowl, as with a little

help beside, served the Company almost a week, at which time amongst other Recreations, we exercised our Arms, many of the Indians coming amongst us, and amongst the rest their greatest king Massasoit, with some ninety men, whom for three days we entertained and feasted, and they went out and killed five Deer, which they brought to the Plantation and bestowed on our Governor, and upon the Captain and others. And although it be not always so plentiful, as it was at this time with us, yet by the goodness of God, we are so far from want, that we often wish you partakers of our plenty.[17]

Virtually everything we know about the real 1621 event comes from this short paragraph. William Bradford's *History of Plymouth Plantation* listed much of the food produced or obtained that summer but does not describe this specific gathering with Indians. A published version of part of Winslow's letter, and Bradford's history, were both lost for a time and not rediscovered until the 1800s, which explains why the 1621 story was unknown earlier and did not become a part of the American historical discussion until that century.

Note several things. First, what Winslow described does not sound like the early Puritan days of thanksgiving for a particular purpose, with a worship service and a family meal. No declaration of a day of thanksgiving, no worship, no prayers are mentioned by Winslow. The recreation with guns, and three days of entertainment in general, would have had no part in a traditional Puritan thanksgiving day, the kind held for a particular reason. This sounds more like the modern American Thanksgiving, with food and festivities, not the early Puritan model. Another way to put it is that it was more like a harvest festival, common in England and in many cultures around the world, than an early Puritan thanksgiving. Second, there is no indication from other sources that the Pilgrims repeated this occasion in the following years as a regular annual event. This apparently was a one-time experience, a celebration of having survived their first winter and summer, rather than the beginning of a tradition for them.

Further, the role of the Native American guests is unclear. Did the Pilgrims invite the Wampanoag ahead of time, for a meal or several days of feasting? Or did the Pilgrim hunters bring in the birds they killed and then begin their sporting recreation, attracting Native Americans curious to see what the noise was about, who then were invited to stay? Or were some Indians invited and already present, and others spontaneously added to their number, wandering in and out? Were the Wampanoag guests, or did they crash the party? Winslow's letter is ambiguous.

In addition, we cannot be certain in what month or on what day this event occurred. Because of the date of Winslow's letter, it must have been prior to December 12. It could have been in September, October, or November.

Some histories say that the Pilgrims and the Wampanoag signed a treaty at this gathering. Winslow's letter says nothing about it. From other historical sources we do know that an alliance was formed between the two groups, but there is no evidence from Winslow that it happened during these three days.

Many additional aspects of the typical Thanksgiving story are questionable. There is no indication that the participants ever sat down for a meal at a table or tables on that day. A shortage of utensils and dishes makes it likelier that food was set out to be picked up and eaten by hand. The clothing worn by the Pilgrims was different from that pictured in traditional illustrations. They did not wear buckles on their hats or on their shoes, because they were too expensive and too much like jewelry. Their clothes might have been black or gray on Sunday, but on other days their clothing could have been yellow, green, brown, or other colors created with natural dyes. Native American clothing is frequently misrepresented as well. Tribes in that region did not wear big headdresses, and in the late fall and winter they wore warm clothing, not loincloths. It also is not true that Indians introduced the Pilgrims to popcorn. The corn available to them did not pop and would probably have been made into a mush.

In sum, some kind of gathering happened at Plymouth in 1621, but the evidence about it is paltry, and even that was lost for about two hundred years. The Thanksgiving story almost all of us learned in school is a creative combination of a tiny bit of history plus legendary additions, an attempt to provide an iconic founding narrative. In the words of Jack Santino, who studies popular culture,

> The first Thanksgiving, the Pilgrims, the fellowship with the Indians, all these have become mythic events in the American consciousness. Historically, there has been a bias toward England as the cultural parent of the United States, and toward New England as the geographical place of origin, despite the fact that it is not the oldest or first area settled, nor were Englishmen the first or only settlers. Nevertheless, the Thanksgiving story has become a kind of origin myth for the United States. It is felt to be the first truly *American* event, and we call the Pilgrims our forefathers.[18]

The appeal of the iconic Thanksgiving story is understandable. It is a tale of survival, of triumph over adversity. It is about people of different cultures meeting in friendship and peace. It is about family, and food, and giving thanks. It provides a foundational national story for reaffirming basic American values. The emergence of the 1621 Pilgrim and Indian story also shifted the emphasis of Sarah Josepha Hale's thanksgiving, at least slightly. It added a historical aspect to what was, for her and many others, a time of giving thanks for present blessings. And it increased the focus on the harvest theme, whereas the colonial New England thanksgiving was a broader transition from fall to winter, an early winter holiday.

DINNER AND MORE

The early Puritan thanksgiving consisted mainly of two things, worship and dinner. Today, for a vast number of Americans Thanksgiving means a dinner, plus parades, football, and the beginning of the Christmas shopping season. Whatever has changed, one striking continuity remains: the family dinner, the core of almost every Thanksgiving celebration. Thanksgiving is not alone as a holiday that gives prominence to a gathering around food. For three of the five holidays considered in this volume, Christmas, Easter /Passover, and Thanksgiving, the dinner is a centerpiece. It should be no surprise that many of our most prominent memories of holidays past include the food we ate, and those with whom we ate it. Food is central to religious practices, in both feasting and fasting, and in general food brings people together. In the words of chef James Beard, "Food is our common ground, a universal experience."[19] For Thanksgiving, as well as the other two holidays, dinner was and is the focal point for family reunions, or when that is not possible, a gathering of friends. As an added feature, in the case of the Thanksgiving dinner, several of the mainstays of today's traditional meal happen to connect directly with the past, with Puritan beginnings. Turkey, cranberries, and pumpkin pie are key parts of the classic traditional American Thanksgiving meal, and all three trace back if not to 1621, at least to the early Puritans.

Turkeys took an interesting route to get to the United States, back and forth across the ocean. They originated in North America, in Mexico, where domesticated turkeys apparently were separated from wild turkeys before the time of Columbus. They were brought to Europe in the 1500s, and some accounts claim they looked very similar to and were confused with a guinea fowl already associated with the country of Turkey, hence the name. In Europe, turkeys and other fowl were more expensive and more prestigious than meat from livestock animals, and they became the featured food for important occasions, including Christmas. After the arrival of turkeys in Europe, they often replaced the goose at special meals, as a step up. When the Plymouth settlers arrived in the New World they encountered wild turkeys in great numbers, but within ten years they had also imported some domestic turkeys from England. Winslow's single paragraph says only that they killed much fowl for their meal in 1621, so that might have included wild turkeys, but it might have been other kinds of birds as well. We do not know. Whether turkeys were consumed at the 1621 meal or not, they were a food Puritans preferred for special occasions and became an expected part of Thanksgiving meals. When wild turkeys were hunted nearly to extinction by the time of the American Revolution, colonists then relied on domestic turkeys.

Pumpkins are a kind of squash, also native to North America. Called "pompion" by the English and in American colonial times (a term meaning squash), they grew easily in New England, on hardy plants requiring little care. Planted in the summer and harvested in the fall, they became associated with both Halloween and Thanksgiving. Pumpkins were an abundant but plain, even bland food, sometimes a staple eaten at almost every meal, boiled, baked, or roasted, usually mashed or pureed. When other crops and food supplies failed, pumpkins were given credit for saving the lives of starving settlers in difficult times. To create a pumpkin pie, however, would require some kind of sweetener, something that may not have been available to the 1621 colonists. Later, when more ingredients were available to whip into a sweetened mixture, the pumpkin pie became a part of the traditional Thanksgiving feast.

Cranberries also were abundant in New England, growing wild on low shrubs with vines trailing along the ground (and later, when domesticated, floating in water bogs). The berries are initially white and turn red as they ripen. The settlers used cranberries as a substitute when their English recipes called for gooseberries or barberries. Barberries, little known today, were similar to cranberries in both their red color and tart flavor, so the native wild cranberries were an ideal replacement. Cranberries were harvested in the late fall when the berries ripened to deep red, anytime from September through November, usually served as a sauce or preserve, and usually sweetened.

Pies of all kinds, both meat pies and sweet desserts, were common in colonial times. On colonial Thanksgiving tables groaning under mountains of food, chicken pies, seldom seen today, stood alongside turkeys as the other standard meat at the meal. Another customary Thanksgiving pie was mincemeat. Recipes from the Middle Ages combined meat with dried fruit, spices, and alcohol, and the combination of added sugars and fermentation made the result sweet enough to become a dessert instead of a main course. Over time the meat was omitted and suet was replaced by vegetable shortening; fruit (raisins, apples, orange and lemon peel, other chopped dried fruit) became the main ingredient, spices (clove, nutmeg, cinnamon, sugar) and wine, brandy, or other spirits were added, and the pie was called a mince pie instead of mincemeat. Until recent decades, mince pies as well as pumpkin pies were the standard dessert choices in many American homes.

From the earliest days, Thanksgiving worship and family feasts included reminders to give to the poor, frequently with food as a focus, to assure that the less fortunate could also have a chance to enjoy a generous meal. Gifts of money were an option, but the charity also might involve personally delivering meals to poor families, or sponsoring occasions where hundreds of the underprivileged ate a meal together. This impulse to generosity was a continuous theme throughout the history of the American Thanksgiving; sometimes the generous deeds were carried out in unassuming fashion, and sometimes they were ostentatious public acts. Historian Diana Karter Appelbaum has described instances in the late 1800s when the affluent "indulged their love of public display by sponsoring elaborate Thanksgiving feasts for the objects of charity. Thanksgiving dinners were given at prisons, almshouses, hospitals, orphanages, settlement houses, and insane asylums amidst great self-congratulation over the fact that on this day no one went hungry. Prisoners at Sing-Sing in New York were regaled with turkey and mince pie and then presented with two cigars each."[20]

Prominent families like the Astors and Vanderbilts, or President Millard Fillmore, or Mrs. Grover Cleveland received publicity for sponsoring charity banquets. Appelbaum also notes that different groups became the focus of attention in different eras; in one period it was children, later it was needy families, and at another time, the elderly. It is possible to be cynical about the motivations behind some of these acts of charity, but it is also true that the spirit of thanksgiving prompted citizens of all walks of life not only to be thankful for their own blessings, but also to think of others, and sometimes the generosity did involve sacrifice. Notice that today, when a family participates in serving a meal at a local food kitchen or a church sponsors a free meal for the community, the Thanksgiving dinner remains at the center of the holiday.

Yet Thanksgiving was about more than eating. Throughout its history, it was a day off work in the middle of a week, something that did not happen often, especially for the working class. What would folks do with the extra time? One early holiday tradition in the United States was, to put it plainly, carousing, in very informal parades where participants, usually drunken men, strolled through the streets celebrating, soliciting food and drink, teasing women, and mocking authority. From the late 1700s and into the next century, something like this occurred in a number of communities and on several holidays. Earlier chapters have mentioned that this behavior was associated with Christmas and Halloween. Other days for such carousing included Washington's Birthday, the Fourth of July, New Year's Eve and New Year's Day, and yes, Thanksgiving.

In the 1800s, especially in New York City and parts of Pennsylvania, these revelers became more organized and were known as Fantastics, or Fantasticals. They paraded in outlandish flamboyant costumes, at times wearing women's clothes, were often accompanied by marching bands, and were clustered into companies or clubs somewhat comparable to New Orleans Mardi Gras krewes, but without the floats. Children costumed like ragamuffins also joined in, begging for money or treats. By the late 1800s, New York parades included more than fifty companies representing different neighborhoods. The parades involved elaborate preparations, plus feasts and balls at the end of the day, and they could be wild. As one newspaper reporter wrote about the participants, "Whether they awake in Police Stations, ash-barrels or in their own beds with their boots on, they will no doubt scratch their heads and wonder whether, after all, 'they had lots of fun on Thanksgiving Day.'"[21] Early in the next century the practice declined and disappeared, the participants pressured by public disapproval of the rowdy behavior and concern that begging was an inappropriate model for children.

In the 1920s, Thanksgiving Day parades returned, but in a new form, sponsored by major department stores. They might have been called Thanksgiving parades, but they really were Christmas parades, because their major purpose was to kick off the Christmas shopping season. That is why department stores sponsored them; there was a reason that Santa Claus almost always appeared at the end, as the culmination of the parade. The first of these annual department store parades took place in 1920 in Philadelphia and was sponsored by Gimbel's. It was followed in 1924 by both the J. L. Hudson parade in Detroit and the Macy's parade in New York City. In its first years the Macy's parade was called the Macy's Christmas Parade, a name that was candid about the parade's emphasis, but in 1927 the name was changed to Macy's Thanksgiving Day Parade. Department stores all over the nation copied these three forerunners with parades of their own, but dropped out in later years when they became too expensive. Commercial or civic groups now sponsor most of the parades in cities such as Chicago, Charlotte, St. Louis, Seattle, and Houston, but the three most prominent are the three oldest, partially because of television coverage. In recent years even the residents of Plymouth, Massachusetts, have added their own Thanksgiving parade, although it takes place on the preceding Saturday. Advertising itself as America's Hometown, Plymouth claims on its website to have "America's only historically accurate chronological parade."

Preeminent among them all is the New York City parade, still sponsored by Macy's. From a beginning with three floats, four bands, and zoo animals, it has grown to include ten thousand participants, over forty giant balloons, many bands and floats, and eight hundred clowns. Over three million people annually fill the city's streets to watch in person, on a parade route forty-three blocks (three and a half miles) long. Additional tens of millions of viewers (Macy's estimate is fifty million) watch the three-hour parade on television. For many families with children, watching the televised parade fills the whole morning.

Another popular option for the use of free time, even in early years, was sport. The 1621 Pilgrim and Indian story itself included shooting guns in some kind of recreation. Over the years the sports have included hunting, sledding, bicycle or foot races, and baseball, but the game that rose to dominance as *the* Thanksgiving sport was football. The American version of football emerged in the mid-1800s. One of the games claimed to be the first college football game was an 1869 contest between Rutgers and the College of New Jersey (now Princeton), although the game as played then looked a lot like rugby. In 1876, a student-organized Intercollegiate Football Association apparently sponsored the first collegiate football game to take place on Thanksgiving Day, and soon thereafter the Ivy League schools began holding their unofficial championship football game, usually between Princeton and Yale, on Thanksgiving Day in New York City. In 1893, 40,000 fans turned out for the game. Thanksgiving rapidly became the designated day for many high school and college football games, especially championships; if they did not take place on the day itself, they were played on the Friday or Saturday following. Even in those years, Thanksgiving football had become so popular that one New York newspaper commentator complained, "Thanksgiving Day is no longer a solemn festival to God for mercies given. . . . It is a holiday granted by the State and the Nation to see a game of football."[22] Why were so many games scheduled for Thanksgiving? As already stated, it was the rare weekday in the fall when vast portions of the population had a day free. College and high school Thanksgiving games have diminished in many parts of the country, now overshadowed by professional football.

THE THANKSGIVING DAY SCRIMMAGE ON BERKELEY OVAL.
THE LIVELY AND INTERESTING BATTLE THAT PRINCETON AND YALE HAD FOR THE FOOTBALL
CHAMPIONSHIP WHEN THE FORMER JUMPED ON THE LATTER.

The intercollegiate championship football game between Princeton and Yale held at
Berkeley Oval, New York, on Thanksgiving Day, 1889, and won by Princeton ten to
nothing. Wood engraving from a contemporary newspaper.

In the first decade of the 1900s, the New York Pro Football League and
the Ohio League, predecessors of today's National Football League (NFL),
held their championship games on Thanksgiving Day, just as the high
schools and colleges were doing. When the NFL started in 1920, it sponsored
six games on Thanksgiving, and through the next two decades many games
continued to be played on that day. In 1934, George A. Richards bought an
Ohio team called the Spartans, moved them to Detroit, and renamed them
the Lions. In that first year he scheduled a game with the Chicago Bears for
Thanksgiving Day, hoping it would help launch his team. It turned out to be
a very successful marketing decision: 28,00 tickets sold out two weeks

before the game. The Lions have played a game on Thanksgiving every year since then, with the exception of 1939-1944, because of changing Thanksgiving dates and World War II. Thereafter the Lions game was featured as the only NFL contest on Thanksgiving (with one exception in 1952) until 1970, when the Dallas Cowboys began to host an annual Thanksgiving game as well. In the first year of the Dallas Thanksgiving game, the league was unsure how many fans would buy tickets and offered the team a minimum guarantee. As it turns out, the league did not have to worry. As had happened in Detroit years earlier, the response in 1970 was overwhelming, setting a new attendance record of over 80,000 spectators in the Cotton Bowl. Of course, the attendance numbers pale in comparison to the number of people listening and watching on radio and television. The games hosted by Detroit and Dallas remained the only two annual NFL Thanksgiving games until 2006. That year the league added a third game, in the evening, featuring different teams each year, and strong television ratings are a clear indication that football on Thanksgiving continues to draw substantial audiences.

So the Thanksgiving Day that once consisted of worship and dinner became instead a dinner with many entertainments and diversions added. What happened to the church services?

Clearly, many Americans still attend worship services on Thanksgiving Eve or Thanksgiving Day, but worship has lost its central position. To paint the transition in very broad strokes, the shift began as far back as the time of the colonial Puritans, when younger generations continued both church attendance and family dinners but tilted the emphasis toward the dinner and family activities. Later, when New Englanders moved into other regions of the new nation and spread their enthusiasm for Thanksgiving, they shared the tradition with Americans who had not been raised with Puritan church backgrounds. These newcomers to Thanksgiving embraced the dinner, the family reunion, and associated amusements, but not so much the extra worship services. Catholic leaders, very aware that Puritans had opposed all things Catholic, initially resisted any kind of observance of the Puritan holy day, although they eventually relented. By the late 1800s even the various Protestant churches had trouble with dwindling attendance on Thanksgiving Day, so they resorted to Union services. Since they knew worship attendance would be small, all Methodist churches in a city, for example, would combine for a single service, hoping that gathering all the small numbers together would assemble a decent-sized congregation. Baptists, Presbyterians, and others did the same thing. In some cities several denominations came together for a single Union service, trying to show unity, as the name suggested, but also attempting to gather a large enough crowd. Today a number of Christian churches provide no worship service at all on Thanksgiving Eve or Day, honoring it as a special time for families to get together. They are content to raise Thanksgiving themes on the Sunday before or after the holiday. It may seem surprising that there is not more outcry from some Christian groups about the diminished role of church services on Thanksgiving Day, but the explanation probably lies in the day's family focus, a value emphasized by those very same groups.

CONTESTED MEANINGS

So Thanksgiving became a national holiday and, like the others, it has become a contested space as participants disagree with one other about its meaning. Three issues arise the most: the role of Native Americans in this story, whether Thanksgiving is a religious or secular holiday, and the impact of commercialization.

Regarding Native Americans and Thanksgiving, most people agree that, however little we know about what happened in 1621, it did appear to be a peaceful interchange across cultures. The concerns are about stereotypes and about tragic events that occurred both before and after the iconic 1621 Plymouth thanksgiving. To reduce stereotypes, in telling the Plymouth story it would be helpful to see the Native American participants as more than just the backdrop to what the Pilgrims did, and a first step is to move beyond generic Indians to understand the particular people involved. When Europeans first came to North America, there were over two hundred different tribes or nations living on the continent (as many as two thousand if you count subgroups), with markedly different languages, housing, clothing, religious beliefs, and so on. The outsiders called them Indians, or later, Native Americans and other alternative terms, but the disadvantage of any general label is that it can lead to oversimplified images that do not recognize the distinctive cultures. The Pilgrims in 1621 did not eat with Native Americans in general; they ate with the Wampanoag people, who lived along what is now the Massachusetts and Rhode Island coast, part of a larger Algonquian-speaking culture in the northeastern woodlands. They lived in round-roofed bark houses called wigwams (not teepees), wore deerskin clothing and fur capes in cold weather, and the men wore a single feather at the back of the head, not full headdresses. The iconic story could be more respectful and meaningful if we learned more about the people and cultures on both sides.

More troubling is the reality that great tragedies occurred both before and after 1621. Waves of smallpox and other diseases ravaged many Native American populations along the East Coast before the Pilgrims arrived, introduced by contact with European explorers and traders. These diseases were devastating to native populations because they had no previous exposure and immunity. A half century after 1621 came what has been called King Philip's War, between Puritan colonists and Native Americans, one of the deadliest wars in American history and one that some activists have described as genocidal. King Philip was a name the English gave to Metacomet, a descendant of the Wampanoag leader Massosoit, who was present at the 1621 gathering. Many Native Americans emphasize that a picture of smiling Indians and colonists in 1621 should not lead us to ignore the difficulties preceding and following the particular event remembered at Thanksgiving.

A number of commentaries and online discussion boards raise a second issue about the meaning of Thanksgiving, asking whether it is a religious or a secular holiday. Advocates on one side quickly point to Thanksgiving's roots in New England Puritanism, origins that focused on thanking God for our blessings. Others highlight Thanksgiving's evolution as a holiday meant to bring the nation together and to include citizens of many religions and no religion; they argue that it is meaningful to set aside a time for thanksgiving wherever the gratitude is directed. This argument is partially an echo of other aspects of the "culture wars" between right and left in today's American society.

Viewed from another angle, it might be helpful to reflect on the different ritual calendars in most Americans' lives, and how those relate to Thanksgiving. Christianity has a ritual calendar, an annual rotation of special times in the year to remember events or reflect on important themes. The two most prominent days in the ritual calendar are Christmas and Easter, but there are many more, especially in "high church" denominations with more ritualized worship. Examples of those special days might be Epiphany, Ash Wednesday, the seasons of Lent and Advent, Pentecost, All Saints' Day, Transfiguration, and more. Other religions have their own ritual calendars as well, including special days such as Rosh Hashanah, Yom Kippur, Sukkot, and Hanukkah in Judaism, the month of Ramadan, the Hajj, and Eid al-Fitr in Islam, and Vesak and Asalha Puja Day in Buddhism. Alongside these religious ritual calendars, most countries have national ritual calendars representing important events in a nation's history or basic themes and values it embraces. In the United States the national ritual calendar consists especially of officially declared federal public holidays, including New Year's Day, Martin Luther King Jr. Day, Washington's Birthday (now Presidents' Day), Memorial Day, Independence Day (the Fourth of July), Labor Day, Columbus Day, Veterans' Day, Thanksgiving, and Christmas. Some additional days are unofficial parts of the national calendar but still very important, like Mother's Day and Father's Day. Some reflect the influence of Christianity as the majority religion, but most do not and are based more on the nation than on religion. I suspect that when most Americans participate in specific religious and national holidays, and I will include myself, we seldom stop to think about them as part of different ritual calendars. There is no need to do so. In our lives they are simply holidays we appreciate and enjoy, and we plunge right in. But when disputes arise, discerning their roots in various ritual calendars can give helpful perspective.

A now-classic academic essay written in the 1960s takes this a bit further. Robert Bellah, a sociologist of religion, argued that the United States does not just have its own ritual calendar; it has its own civil religion. Bellah argued that "there actually exists alongside of and rather clearly differentiated from the churches an elaborate and well-institutionalized civil religion in America." He called it a civil religion because it has many of the forms common in other religions but is centered on the nation: "It has its own prophets and its own martyrs, its own sacred events and sacred places, its own solemn rituals and symbols."[23] Bellah did not think the United States was alone in this; he felt that many nations have something similar. If this is the way to describe an American civil religion, it is easy to fill in examples: symbols (the American flag, the Liberty Bell, the bald eagle), sacred scriptures (the Declaration of Independence and the Constitution), pilgrimage sites and shrines (Washington, DC, Mount Vernon, Gettysburg), prophets (George Washington, Thomas Jefferson), martyrs (Abraham Lincoln, Martin Luther King Jr.), central shared beliefs (freedom, equality, a divine purpose for the nation), and sacred events and rituals (election day, inaugurations, and the entire ritual calendar of national holidays remembering sacred history, people, and values). As you might guess, over the years scholars have debated this idea of an American civil religion. Is it actually a religion, or is it just *similar* to a religion? Should more traditional religions like Judaism and Christianity see a national civil religion as a rival, or can they be combined? Good questions.

In light of this talk about an American civil religion, the question about Thanksgiving is not just whether it is secular or religious but also, if it is religious, to which religion does it belong?

A third issue about Thanksgiving is commercialization, a topic mentioned in connection with every one of the five holidays included in this book. The dramatic difference in this case is that a discussion of the commercialization of Thanksgiving is not about how much money is spent or how many products are sold for Thanksgiving itself. It is about Thanksgiving as the gateway to the Christmas shopping season. As an experiment, try an online word search for the "commercialization of Thanksgiving." Almost every single result is about Christmas sales starting before Thanksgiving, or on Thanksgiving, or about Black Friday, but almost nothing focuses on spending *for Thanksgiving.* As another experiment, in November walk into a store like Target or Walmart in search of a centerpiece for a Thanksgiving dinner table. What will you find? Almost nothing.

Of course there is some commercial activity for Thanksgiving purposes, although little to compare with the other four holidays. Most is for food and travel. The Sunday after Thanksgiving is the heaviest airline travel day of the year in the United States, and the Wednesday before is likewise among the busiest, an indication of Thanksgiving's importance as a homecoming celebration. In terms of food, approximately one-sixth of the turkey sold in the United States is consumed at Thanksgiving, and one-fifth of the cranberries are consumed in Thanksgiving week. The National Turkey Federation has estimated that Americans eat 45 million turkeys at Thanksgiving, compared to 22 million at Christmas and 19 million at Easter. The other food items most often purchased for Thanksgiving are pies.

Yet the main story is about what the commercialization of Christmas is doing to Thanksgiving, something that has been building for a century. After all, it was in the 1920s that the Thanksgiving Day department store parades began, and even then they were more about Santa Claus than

Thanksgiving. Only a couple of decades later, Christmas economics prompted a change in the very date of Thanksgiving. By that time the day after Thanksgiving had become known as the start of the Christmas shopping season, for quite obvious and logical reasons. Thanksgiving was the last major holiday prior to Christmas, so with that special day out of the way, Americans could turn their attention to the next one. In addition, many governments and businesses gave their employees the day off on Friday, creating a long holiday weekend and giving a huge portion of the population some time to begin their Christmas shopping. The phrase "Black Friday" was first coined by the Philadelphia police in the 1960s, as a negative term to describe the heavy traffic and bad behavior that began right after Thanksgiving: traffic jams, crowds of shoppers trampling one another in order to grab featured bargains, and lots of angry people. The chaos was especially pronounced in Philadelphia because that city also hosted the annual Army-Navy football game on Thanksgiving Saturday. It was a difficult day and weekend for Philadelphia police, and the derogatory name Black Friday seemed appropriate. In the 1970s, however, the popular meaning of the phrase shifted to something very different, a reference to business profits. In accounting language, where "in the red" means being in debt and "in the black" means making a profit, the Friday after Thanksgiving became known as the day when businesses could break even and start making a profit for the remainder of the year because of consumer Christmas spending.

Merchants in recent years have tried to gain a competitive advantage by beginning their Christmas sales as early as possible, opening at 6:00 or even 4:00 on the morning of Black Friday. In 2011 some retailers opened at midnight, and one year later several stores began opening on Thanksgiving Day itself, crossing the line into a Thursday that had previously been considered sacrosanct by many. Retail employees complained that opening stores on Thanksgiving Day deprived them of an evening with their families, and others resented the attempt to lure customers away from their homes on such a special day. Social media campaigns emerged to "Stop Black Thursday" or "Boycott Black Thanksgiving." One protester commented about the entire drift, "It is pathetic that our consumer-driven economy worships the dollar over people."[24] Such complaints have been common throughout American history as virtually every holiday has felt the impact of commercial developments, but the changes continue.

It is increasingly common to bemoan the commercial onslaught surrounding Thanksgiving and to fear for the future of the holiday, sandwiched as it is between the overwhelmingly popular Halloween and Christmas. Considering these challenges, I find the tenacity of Thanksgiving to be remarkable. So much travel and so much turkey indicate a continuing public affection for Thanksgiving, even when it seems to be under threat of being totally swallowed up by adjacent holidays. Thanksgiving seems to be more than just surviving; in a recent Harris Poll asking Americans about their favorite holidays, Thanksgiving came in second only to Christmas, in all categories of the population.[25] Whatever the additions and distractions over the years, the heart of the day remains a homecoming, a meal with family and friends, and a time set aside to be thankful. Even those who are unable to participate in a given year often reflect on memories of food and traditions and hope to be part of such a gathering again in the future, maybe next year. Thanksgiving touches an elemental yearning for home and family that competition and controversies have been unable to extinguish.

Afterword

There they are, candid histories of five of the most popular holidays in the United States. What can a person do with this information, in addition to sharing interesting factoids with friends? It is said that history answers five basic questions (what, who, when, where, and why), but I once had a history professor who claimed there were really only two questions: what, and so what. I am not so sure, because I hesitate to claim that historical narratives offer obvious lessons or morals of the story. Yet the information in those narratives, and the interpretations of them, can certainly provide starting points for personal reflection. Let me suggest two possibilities.

What does the popularity of these holidays say about American culture, and about me? As mentioned near the end of the Valentine's Day chapter, a basic principle when analyzing popular culture is that popular culture both influences *and* reflects us. It certainly is true that advertisers, business interests, celebrities, movie and television producers, and other key cultural decision makers can wield great influence in shaping society for good or ill, promoting or discouraging viewpoints and behaviors. Yet we in the public are not simply their pawns, powerless to resist their manipulation. While these cultural authorities are a shaping force, we influence them in return every time we purchase or ignore a product, attend an event, or watch a television program. Movies, food products, and clothing fashions are introduced regularly, with heavy advertising, and a high percentage of them fail because the general public is not interested in them. The public and producers influence each other in a sort of constant feedback loop. Where the commercialization of holidays is concerned, it's easy to complain that "they" have commercialized the holidays, as if we in the general public played no role—but we *do* play one.

So it's worth asking, in the case of each holiday considered in this book, why is it so popular? What does it say about American society? What needs does it fill? What hopes or yearnings are revealed there? More personally, what is my favorite holiday, and *why* is it my favorite? It is an opportunity to learn about ourselves, individually and collectively.

Which of the three possible functions of holidays are most important to me? In the introduction, I suggested that holidays might serve three possible functions for individuals: recommitment, relaxation, and release. A particular holiday might give us the opportunity to recommit ourselves to our loved ones, to God or our religion, or to our nation. A holiday might also give us a break, time to relax and back away from pressures, time to recuperate and renew. It might also give us a chance to let go, to party, to release ourselves from some of the restrictions that inhibit us in daily life. I suspect that most of us need all three at one time or another.

The possibility here is to look at each holiday individually and ask which function, or which combination, is most important to you. The answer is likely to be different for each holiday. When I feel frustrated about certain holidays, I find this technique helpful in diagnosing my dissatisfaction and deciding how I want to shift my emphasis in order to get a different result. Too often, when we approach a holiday we simply go on autopilot, but we do have choices, and this kind of reflection can help reveal them.

Holidays meet a need in us—they appeal to a dream, or satisfy a yearning. They are like a mirror, reflecting back to us our culture and sometimes our individual selves. When we look in that mirror, we see memories we cherish and traditions that give rhythm to our lives. Most important of all, when we take time to think about our celebrations and motivations, we see ourselves.

NOTES

INTRODUCTION

1. https://nrf.com/news/the-long-and-short-of-americas-consumer-holidays, accessed 2/28/15. Also high on the list of consumer spending are Mother's Day and Father's Day, which are worthy of consideration but not part of this project.

2. Charles M. Schultz, *Peanuts, Holidays through the Year: Five Classic Stories* (Philadelphia: Running Press for Hallmark Cards, 2007).

3. Bill Nichols, "The Christmas Classic That Almost Wasn't," *USA Today*, Dec. 5, 2005.

4. Amitai Etzioni, "Holidays and Rituals: Neglected Seedbeds of Virtue," in *We Are What We Celebrate: Understanding Holidays and Rituals*, ed. Amitai Etzioni and Jared Bloom (New York: New York University Press, 2004), 12.

1. CHRISTMAS

1. This chapter, although reshaped, is a distillation of information from my book *Christmas: A Candid History* (Berkeley: University of California Press, 2007) and a spin-off article, "Christmas Was Not Always Like This: A Brief History," *Word & World* 27:4 (Fall 2007), 399–406.

2. All biblical quotations in this volume are from the New Revised Standard Version (NRSV) translation.

3. Thomas J. Talley, *The Origins of the Liturgical Year*, 2nd ed. (Collegeville, MN: Liturgical Press, 1991), 103–121; Roland H. Bainton, "The Origins of Epiphany," in *Studies in Early Christianity: A Collection of Scholarly Essays*, vol. 15, ed. Everett Ferguson (New York: Garland, 1993).

4. Susan K. Roll, *Toward the Origins of Christmas* (Kampen, Netherlands: Kok Pharos, 1995), 83–86.

5. Stephen Nissenbaum, *The Battle for Christmas* (New York: Alfred A. Knopf, 1996), 7–8.

6. Bertram Colgrave and R. A. B. Rynors, eds., *Bede's Ecclesiastical History of the English People* (Oxford: Clarendon Press, 1969), 107, 109.

7. www.aboutflowers.com/flower-holidays-occasions-a-parties/christmas/christmas-statistics.html, accessed 1/22/15.

8. Michael Patrick Hearn, introduction to Charles Dickens, *The Annotated Christmas Carol: A Christmas Carol in Prose* (New York: W. W. Norton, 2004), xv.

9. Tom Flynn, *The Trouble with Christmas* (Buffalo, NY: Prometheus Books, 1993), 88.

10. J. M. Golby and A. W. Purdue, *The Making of the Modern Christmas* (Athens: University of Georgia Press, 1986), 36, 40, 44.

11. Quoted by Robert Doares, "Colonial Church Christmases," *Colonial Williamsburg* (Christmas 2005), 29.

12. Karal Ann Marling, *Merry Christmas! Celebrating America's Greatest Holiday* (Cambridge, MA: Harvard University Press, 2000), 137.

13. James H. Barnett, *The American Christmas: A Study in National Culture* (New York: Macmillan, 1954), 14.

14. Stanley Weintraub, *Albert: Uncrowned King* (London: John Murray, 1997), 114.

15. Asa Briggs, *The Age of Improvement, 1783–1867* (London: Longmans, 1959), 447.

16. Chapter 4 in *Christmas: A Candid History* adds many details to this summary.

17. Tanya Gulevich, *Encyclopedia of Christmas* (Detroit: Ominigraphics, 2000), 147–149; www.newdream.org, accessed 7/20/06.

2. VALENTINE'S DAY

1. Plutarch, *Lives, Volume 1*, trans. Bernadotte Perrin, Loeb Classical Library 46 (Cambridge, MA: Harvard University Press, 1914), 157–159.

2. Tertullian, *Apology,* ch 50, 13, various editions and translations.

3. Jack B. Oruch, "St. Valentine, Chaucer, and Spring in February," *Speculum* 56:3 (July 1981), 535. Much of the information about Valentine in the following paragraphs relies on this article.

4. Oruch, 536.

5. *Calendarium Romanum* (Libreria Editrice Vaticana, 1969), 117.

6. Gelasius, quoted in Mary Beard, John North, and Simon Price, eds., *Religions of Rome, Volume 2: A Sourcebook* (New York: Cambridge University Press, 1998), 123.

7. Summarized by William M. Green, "The Lupercalia in the Fifth Century," *Classical Philology* 26:1 (Jan. 1931), 60–69.

8. Green, 61. Oruch, 540–541.

9. Oruch, 539–540.

10. Andreas Capellanus, *The Art of Courtly Love*, trans. and ed. John Jay Parry (New York: Columbia University Press, 1989), 81.

11. Ruth M. Ames, *God's Plenty: Chaucer's Christian Humanism* (Chicago: Loyola University Press, 1984), 113.

12. C.S. Lewis, *The Allegory of Love: A Study in Medieval Tradition* (London: Oxford University Press, 1936), 161, 174.

13. Norman E. Eliason, "Chaucer the Love Poet," in *Chaucer the Love Poet*, eds. Jerome Mitchell and William Provost (Athens: University of Georgia Press, 1973), 9.

14. Geoffrey Chaucer, *The Parlament of Foules*, ed. T.R. Lounsbury (Boston: Ginn and Heath, 1878), 65.

15. Modern translation by A.S. Kline, www.poetryintranslation.com /PITBR/English/Fowls.htm, accessed 3/1/15.

16. Oruch, 565. Henry Ansgar Kelly, *Chaucer and the Cult of Saint Valentine* (Leiden: E.J. Brill, 1986).

17. Oruch, 565.

18. Kelly, 76–127.

19. Oruch, 559.

20. www.bl.uk/learning/timeline/large126579.html, accessed 2/1/14.

21. Samuel Woodworth, "Appendix: American Festivals, Games, and Amusements," in Horatio Smith, *Festivals, Games, and Amusements* (New York: Harper and Brothers, 1832), 334–335. Quoted in Leigh Eric Schmidt, *Consumer Rites: The Buying and Selling of American Holidays* (Princeton: Princeton University Press, 1995), 49.

22. London and New York statistics quoted by Schmidt, 49–50.

23. Letter to William Cowper Dickinson, Feb. 14, 1849, in Emily Dickinson, *Emily Dickinson: Selected Letters*, ed. Thomas Herbert Johnson (Cambridge: Harvard University Press / Belknap Press, 1986), 30.

24. *Rauner Library Blog*, http://raunerlibrary.blogspot.com/2012_02_12_archive.html, accessed 2/8/14.

25. Schmidt, 77.

26. Schmidt, 96–97.

27. Notable Names Database, www.nndb.com/people/270/000164775/, accessed 2/7/14.

28. "Consumers Keep Budgets in Check This Valentine's Day, According to NRF," National Retail Federation press release, Feb. 4, 2014.

29. www.fierceretail.com/story/four-retail-trends-valentines-day/2014-02-07, accessed 2/8/14.

30. Martin Kemp, *Christ to Coke: How Image Becomes Icon* (New York: Oxford University Press, 2012), 85.

31. Kemp, 99–100, 105.

32. Kemp, 110.

33. Ole M. Hoystad, *A History of the Heart* (London: Reaktion Books, 2007), 126.

3. EASTER

1. Tamara Prosic, *The Development and Symbolism of Passover until 70 CE* (London/New York: T & T Clark International, 2004), 32.

2. Theodor Herzl Gaster, *Passover: Its History and Traditions* (New York: Henry Schuman, 1949), 16–17, 21.

3. James VanderKam, "Passover and Feast of Unleavened Bread," in *The New Interpreter's Dictionary of the Bible*, ed. Katharine Doob Sakenfeld et al. (Nashville: Abingdon Press, 2009), vol. 4, 388–392.

4. Morris N. Kertzer and Lawrence A. Hoffman, *What Is a Jew?* (New York: Simon & Schuster / Touchstone, 1993 rev. ed.), 225.

5. Paul F. Bradshaw and Maxwell E. Johnson, *The Origins of Feasts, Fasts and Seasons in Early Christianity* (Collegeville, MN: Liturgical Press, 2011), chap. 5.

6. Faith Wallis, trans., *Bede: The Reckoning of Time* (Liverpool: Liverpool University Press, 1999), 54.

7. Joan Acocella, "Once Upon a Time: The Lure of the Fairy Tale," *New Yorker,* July 23, 2012, www.newyorker.com/magazine/2012/07/23/once-upon-a-time-3.

8. Jacob Grimm, *Teutonic Mythology: Translated from the Fourth Edition with Notes and Appendix,* trans. James Steven Stallybrass, vol. 1 (London: George Bell and Sons, 1882), 290.

9. www.bio.miami.edu/hare/scary.pdf, accessed 10/29/14.

10. Alfred Lewis Shoemaker, *Eastertide in Pennsylvania: A Folk-Cultural Study* (Mechanicsburg, PA: Stackpole Books, 2000 [1960]), 45.

11. Westminster Assembly, *Directory for Publick Worship* (1645).

12. *New-York Daily Tribune,* Apr. 13, 1868.

13. Tanya Gulevich, *Encyclopedia of Easter, Carnival and Lent* (Detroit: Omnigraphics, 2002), 518–519.

14. Venetia Newell, "Easter Eggs," *Journal of American Folklore* 80:315 (Jan.-Mar. 1967), 3–8.

15. Venetia Newell, "Easter Eggs: Symbols of Life and Renewal," *Folklore* 95:1 (1984), 21.

16. Newell, "Easter Eggs: Symbols," 19.

17. David Ng, "Flea Market Find: Faberge Egg for $14,000, May Be Worth $33 Million," *Los Angeles Times,* Mar. 20, 2014.

18. Gary Cross, *The Cute and the Cool: Wondrous Innocence and Modern American Children's Culture* (New York: Oxford University Press, 2004), 100.

19. Steve Olenski, "The Ups and Downs of Marketing during Easter 2014," www.forbes.com/sites/steveolenski/2014/04/14/the-ups-and-downs-of-marketing-during-easter-2014/, accessed 11/6/14.

20. National Retail Federation press release, "Consumers Hope to Shake Off Winter Blues This Easter, According to NRF," https://nrf.com/media/press-

releases/consumers-hope-shake-winter-blues-this-easter-according-nrf, accessed 11/6/2014.

21. Barna Group, "Most Americans Consider Easter a Religious Holiday, but Fewer Correctly Identify Its Meaning," www.barna.org/barna-update /culture/356-most-americans-consider-easter-a-religious-holiday-but-fewer-correctly-identify-its-meaning, accessed 11/6/14.

22. *Dry Goods Economist*, Mar. 24, 1894, 36, 37, quoted by Leigh Eric Schmidt, *Consumer Rites: The Buying and Selling of American Holidays* (Princeton: Princeton University Press, 1995), 213.

23. Peter Steinfels, "Sacred and Secular in Easter Celebrations: Family Holiday Isn't What It Used to Be," *New York Times*, Mar. 23, 1988.

4. HALLOWEEN

1. David J. Skal, *Death Makes a Holiday: A Cultural History of Halloween* (New York: Bloomsbury, 2002), 21.

2. Lisa Morton, *Trick or Treat: A History of Halloween* (London: Reaktion Books, 2012), 9–11.

3. Julius Caesar, *The Gallic War*, ed. H. J. Edward (London: Loeb, 1986), 341.

4. Nicholas Rogers, *Halloween: From Pagan Ritual to Party Night* (New York: Oxford University Press, 2002), 14.

5. Ole J. Benedictow, "The Black Death: The Greatest Catastrophe Ever," *History Today* 55:3 (Mar. 2005).

6. Morton, 21.

7. John Demos, *The Enemy Within: Two Thousand Years of Witch-Hunting in the Western World* (New York: Viking/Penguin, 2008), 63–64.

8. Demos, 38–39.

9. Christopher S. Mackey, *The Hammer of Witches: A Complete Translation of the "Malleus Maleficarum"* (New York: Cambridge University Press, 2009). Mackey actually is the translator. Heinrich Kramer and Jacob Sprenger, both inquisitors at witch trials, traditionally are listed as the authors.

10. Thomas Christopher Smout, *A History of the Scottish People 1560–1830* (Fontana/Collins, 1987 rev. ed.), 198–207.

11. Rogers, 50.

12. Kerby A. Miller, *Emigrants and Exiles: Ireland and the Irish Exodus to North America* (New York: Oxford University Press, 1985), 346.

13. www.phrases.org.uk/meanings/trick-or-treat.html, accessed 12/16/14, citing *The Oregon Journal*, Nov. 1, 1934, and *The Vidette-Messenger*, Oct. 30, 1937.

14. "Past Halloween Pranks Bemused Some and Frustrated Others," http://connecticuthistory.org/past-halloween-pranks-bemused-some-and-frustrated-others/, accessed 12/26/14.

15. "Halloween," in Robert Burns, *Poems, Chiefly in the Scottish Dialect* (New York: AMS Press, 1974 facsimile ed.), 105–106.

16. Lesley Pratt Bannatyne, *Halloween: An American Holiday, an American History* (Gretna, Louisiana: Pelican Publishing, 2005), 77.

17. Skal, 20.

18. Lettie C. VanDerveer, *Halloween Happenings* (Boston: W. H. Baker, 1921), 14. Quoted in Rogers, 77.

19. Rogers, 67.

20. Ruth Edna Kelley, *The Book of Hallowe'en* (n.p.: Better Days Books, 2011 [1919]), 115.

21. June Anderson, "Anoka County History: Halloween Capital of the World," Oct. 25, 2012, http://abcnewspapers.com/2012/10/25/anoka-county-history-halloween-capital-of-the-world/, accessed 12/14/14.

22. Tad Tuleja, "Trick or Treat: Pre-texts and Contexts," in *Halloween and Other Festivals of Death and Life*, ed. Jack Santino (Knoxville: University of Tennessee Press, 1994), 89.

23. Morton, 83.

24. Michael Winerip, "At Halloween, Unicef Faces Declining Collections in U.S.," *New York Times*, Oct. 31, 1993.

25. Joel Best, "Halloween Sadism: The Evidence," www.udel.edu/soc/faculty/best/site/halloween.html, accessed 12/28/14.

26. www.loc.gov/programs/national-film-preservation-board/film-registry/complete-national-film-registry-listing/descriptions-and-essays/, accessed 1/5/14.

27. Bruce Horowitz, "Scary! Halloween's Been Hijacked by Adults," *USA Today*, Oct. 24, 2012, www.spirithalloween.com/about-spirit/, accessed 1/6/14.

28. Kerry Wills and Mike Jaccarino, "Greenwich Village Halloween Parade Thrills Costume-Clad Crowd," *New York Daily News*, Oct. 31, 2011.

29. Horowitz.

30. https://nrf.com/news/the-long-and-short-of-americas-consumer-holidays, accessed 2/28/15.

31. Tim Burton, *Burton on Burton*, ed. Mark Salisbury (London: Faber and Faber, 2006 rev. ed.), 124.

32. Elizabeth Carmichael and Chloe Sayer, *The Skeleton at the Feast: The Day of the Dead in Mexico* (Austin: University of Texas Press, 1991), 28.

5. THANKSGIVING

1. H.L. Mencken, *A Mencken Chrestomathy* (New York: Vintage / Random House, 1982), 624.

2. James W. Baker, *Thanksgiving: The Biography of an American Holiday* (Durham: University of New Hampshire Press, 2009), 17-23.

3. Albert Matthews, "The Term *Pilgrim Fathers* and Early Celebrations of Forefathers' Day," in *Publications of the Colonial Society of Massachusetts* (Boston: The Society), vol. 17 (1915):293-391.

4. Baker, 36-37.

5. Diana Karter Appelbaum, *Thanksgiving: An American Holiday, an American History* (New York: Facts on File, 1984), 48.

6. Appelbaum, 57.

7. Letter from Thomas Jefferson to Reverend Samuel Miller, Jan. 23, 1808, in Thomas Jefferson, *Memoir, Correspondence, and Miscellanies: From the Papers of Thomas Jefferson* (F. Carr and Company, 1829), vol. 4, 104.

8. Appelbaum, 94.

9. *Milwaukee Sentinel*, Dec. 25, 1838.

10. Abby Goodnough, "Living History at National Monuments: Championing an Unsung Hero," *New York Times*, July 4, 2010, national section, 10.

11. Quoted in Baker, 72.

12. "Landon Calls It Hitler Tactics," *St. Petersburg Times*, Aug. 17, 1939, 1.

13. Quoted in Penny Colman, *Thanksgiving: The True Story* (New York: Henry Holt, 2008), 62, 49.

14. Robert Tracy McKenzie, *The First Thanksgiving* (Downers Grove, IL: Inter-Varsity Press, 2013), 149, 152.

15. For lists of the possibilities, see Colman, 9–24, and Baker, 8.

16. Jane Cobb, "Living and Leisure: Thanksgiving," *Washington Post*, Nov. 17, 1940.

17. Modern spelling from the Pilgrim Hall Museum, www.pilgrimhallmuseum .org/pdf/TG_What_Happened_in_1621.pdf, accessed 3/1/15.

18. Jack Santino, *All around the Year: Holidays and Celebrations in American Life* (Urbana: University of Illinois Press, 1994), 175.

19. James Beard, *Beard on Food: The Best Recipes and Kitchen Wisdom from the Dean of American Cooking* (New York: Bloomsbury, 2008), xi.

20. Appelbaum, 178.

21. Quoted in Appelbaum, 190.

22. Baker, 76.

23. Robert N. Bellah, *Beyond Belief: Essays on Religion in a Post-traditional World* (New York: Harper & Row, 1970), 168, 186. His essay "Civil Religion in America" was published first in *Daedalus* in 1966.

24. Hadley Malcolm and Oliver St. John, "Retail Employees Rebel against Early Black Fridays," *USA Today*, Nov. 20, 2012.

25. www.prnewswire.com/news-releases/happy-holidays--christmas-is-americas-favorite-holiday-131577758.html, accessed 1/22/15.

chestnuts, 132
Chicago Bears, 182–83
Chicago (IL), 180
chicken pie, 178
China, 101, 105
chocolate, 110
Christianity: accommodation with native traditions, 23–26; annual ritual calendar in, 89–92, 186; baptism in, 104; communion in, 88; conservative, and Halloween, 117, 143–44; Easter as most important holiday in, 79; spread of, 22–26; as US culturally dominant religion, 6
Christianity, early: birthdays uncelebrated in, 20; Easter emphasized in, 18, 19; Jesus nativity celebrations absent in, 3, 10, 17–18; martyrdom in, 18, 20, 48–50, 119–20
Christianity, eastern, 19, 80, 120
Christine de Pizan, 61
Christmas: Advent as leadup period to, 22; on annual Christian ritual calendar, 89; beginnings of, 17–22; childhood memories of, 2; Christian overlay, 16–17, 19–22, 43; Christian vs. cultural, 42–43; commercialization of, 13 *fig.*, 35, 39, 41–42, 43, 70, 72, 73, 115–16, 148, 167, 168, 188–90; date of, 90, 97–99; domestication of, 4, 34–35, 43, 139; early marketing/decorating for, 115–16; as floral-buying holiday, 25–26; food at, 176, 188; functions of, 43; German traditions, 130; gifts during, 41–42; "Keep Christ in Christmas" campaigns, 21–22, 45; as national holiday, 186; New Testament mentions of, 18–19; popularity of, 190; Puritan suppression of, 27–29; as recommitment celebration, 148–49;

revival of, 29–35, 31 *fig.*, 33 *fig.*; Santa Claus/St. Nicholas and, 13 *fig.*, 35–40, 36 *fig.*, 38 *fig.*, 40 *fig.*, 69; shopping season for, 167, 168, 175, 180, 188–90; spread of, as snowball process, 23–26; theoretical frameworks for understanding, 14, 43, 148–49; Twelve Days of, 22; use of term, 23; US popularity of, 13; as winter celebration, 9, 14–17, 43, 97–99
Christmas: A Candid History (Forbes), 3
Christmas cards, 41, 70
Christmas Carol, A (Dickens), 29–32, 31 *fig.*, 41, 42
Christmas spirit, 32, 42
Christmas trees, 16, 26, 32–34, 33 *fig.*, 41
Chronograph of 354, 19, 52
Church, Francis, 39
Church of England, 29, 154–55, 156, 158. *See also* Anglican Church
Church of Scotland, 28
circle, as general symbol, 105
civil religion, 6, 66, 171, 187–88
Civil War, 165, 169
Clanvowe, John, 61
Claudius I (Roman emperor), 51–52
Claudius II (Roman emperor), 51–52
Clement VII, Pope, 154
Cleveland, Mrs. Grover, 178
clothing, 1–2, 72, 110–13, 114, 114 *fig.*
Coca-Cola, 13 *fig.*, 39
College of New Jersey, 181. *See also* Princeton University
Colman, Penny, 168
Columbus Day, 186
commercialization: of Christmas, 13 *fig.*, 35, 39, 41–42, 43, 70, 72, 73, 115–16, 148, 167, 168, 188–90; of Easter, 5, 110–14, 113 *fig.*, 114 *fig.*, 148; of Halloween, 70, 72, 73, 110, 115–16, 139, 146, 147–48; of Thanksgiving, 5,

Oktoberfest, 8
Old Testament, 86
Olenski, Steve, 110
Oregon, 131
Oruch, Jack, 50, 54, 60
Oschter Haws (Easter hare), 102
Ostara (Germanic deity), 96
Osterhase (Easter hare), 102
Oton de Granson, 61
Ovid, 48
owls, 136

paganism/pagans, 16, 17, 53–54, 116
Palm Sunday, 97
Paris, Treaty of (1783), 159
Parliament of Fowls, The (Chaucer), 58–60, 62
Passover, 6; Easter as Christian celebration of, 80–81, 86–93, 98 *fig.*; food at, 176; Jewish observance of, 81–86, 85 *fig.*, 105, 113–14
Paston, John, 63
Patrick, Saint, 119
Paul, Saint, 18, 19
Peanuts (comic strip), 5
peer pressure, 78
Pennsylvania, 161, 164
Pentecost, 89, 186
I Peter, Epistle of, 89
Peter, Paul and Mary (folk group), 129–30
Peterson, Cassandra, 147
Philadelphia (PA), 112, 141, 180, 189
Philocalian Calendar, 19, 52
Phocas (Roman emperor), 120
Pierce, Franklin, 164
pies, 176, 177–78, 188
Pilgrims, 153–54, 153 *fig.*, 156, 169–73, 172 *fig.*, 184–85. *See also* Puritanism/Puritans
Pilgrim's Progress (Bunyan), 162

Pintard, John, 36 *fig.*, 37
pisanki (decorated eggs), 107
plague, 115 *fig.*, 122–23, 124
Playboy bunnies, 101
Plutarch, 47–48
Plymouth Colony, 157, 169–71
Plymouth (MA), 180
"Plymouth Oration" (Webster), 170
Plymouth Rock (MA), 153
Plymouth Society, 170
poinsettias, 25–26
Poinsett, Joel Roberts, 25
Poland, 106, 107
Pontius Pilate, 106
popcorn, 174
popular culture, modern, 9, 43, 78, 191–92
Potter, Beatrix, 103
Presbyterianism, 27, 28, 102, 184
Presidents' Day, 186
Princeton University, 181, 182 *fig. 2*
Protestantism, 184; Easter celebrations in, 91, 92
Protestant Reformation, 122, 124
Pumphrey, Margaret, 171
pumpkin pie, 177
pumpkins, 10, 129, 133, 177
Purdue, William, 27
Purim, 8
Puritanism/Puritans: Catholic beliefs/practices opposed by, 102, 154–55, 183–84; Christmas celebrations opposed by, 27–29, 30, 154; Easter celebrations opposed by, 101–2, 154; emigration to New World, 156–57, 169, 172; separating vs. non-separating, 156–57, 172; Thanksgiving origins in, 154–58. *See also* Pilgrims
Puritan Revolution, 27
pysanki (decorated eggs), 107, 108 *fig.*

Index

United Nations International Children's Emergency Fund (UNICEF), 141

United States: Christianity as culturally dominant religion in, 6; Christmas commercialization in, 41–42; Christmas revival in, 29–30, 31 *fig.*; Christmas suppressed in, 26–27, 28–29, 102; civil religion in, 6, 66, 187–88; culturally dominant holidays in, 4–6, 13, 190; Day of the Dead in, 151–52; Dickens tours in, 29–30; Easter egg imagery in, 109–10; Easter suppressed in, 101–2; emigration to, 127–28; Halloween brought to, 127–28; Halloween opposed in, 117, 143–44; Halloween traditions in, 127–37; Hispanic population in, 152; national ritual calendar of, 171, 186–87; Puritanism in, 28–29, 101–2; religious/cultural pluralism in, 26; Santa Claus as creation of, 39–40; Thanksgiving story as origin myth of, 175; Valentine's Day observance in, 66–68, 69–73; witch hunts in, 127, 171

United States Congress, 159–60, 168

United States Film Registry, 145

University of Kansas, 60

University of Miami, 100

valentine cards, 45, 65, 66–73, 67 *fig.*, 71 *fig.*

Valentine of Genoa, Saint, 60–61

Valentine, Saint, 46–47, 48–52, 49 *fig.*, 64–65

Valentine's Day: childhood memories of, 2; Christian overlay on, 10, 46–47, 48–52, 49 *fig.*, 64–65; commercialization of, 65–73, 67 *fig.*, 71 *fig.*, 78, 148; conventional history of origin of, 46–55, 60; courtly love and

beginnings of, 55–65, 57 *fig.*; date of, 60–61; engagements occurring on, 1, 73, 148; English observances of, 27–28, 66; as floral-buying holiday, 25; heart symbol on, 46, 73–78, 77 *fig.*; as holiday, 11; love birds and, 58–60, 62; as recommitment celebration, 149; as spring celebration, 9, 10, 46–47, 60–61; theoretical frameworks for understanding, 149; US observances of, 66–68

valentines (poems), 61–63

"Valentine Writers," 68–69

Vallancey, Charles, 117

Vancouver (WA), 147

Vanderbilt family, 178

Varro (Roman scholar), 48

Vassar College, 162

Vatican II (1969), 52

Velveteen Rabbit, The (Williams), 103

Vesak, 186

Veterans' Day, 186

Victoria, Queen of England, 26, 29, 32, 33 *fig.*

Village Halloween Parade (New York, NY), 146–47

Virginia, 170

Virgin Mary, 75

Visit from St. Nicholas, A (poem; Moore), 38 *fig.*

Wales, 116, 128

Wampanoag people, 185

War of 1812, 160

washings, ritual, 104–5

Washington, George, 159, 160, 162

Washington's birthday, 66, 165, 171, 179, 186

water, as general symbol, 104–5

Watership Down (Adams), 104